From Foe to Friend

One Man's Experience in Japanese/American Trade

Shinsaku Sogo

with Bill Hosokawa

Fulcrum Publishing
Golden, Colorado

Library of Congress Cataloging-in-Publication Data
Sogo, Shinsaku.
From foe to friend : one man's experience in Japanese/American trade / Shinsaku Sogo, with Bill Hosokawa.
p. cm.
ISBN 1-55591-459-4
1. Sogo, Shinsaku. 2. Businessmen—Japan—Biography. 3. Foreign trade promotion—Japan. 4. United States—Foreign economic relations—Japan—Congresses. 5. Japan—Foreign economic relations—United States—Congresses. I. Hosokawa, Bill. II. Title.
HC461.5.S67 S67 2002
382'.0952073—dc21

2002000464

Book and jacket design by Patty Maher

Printed in the United States of America
0 9 8 7 6 5 4 3 2 1

Fulcrum Publishing
16100 Table Mountain Parkway, Suite 300
Golden, Colorado 80403
(800) 992-2908 • (303) 277-1623
www.fulcrum-books.com

To Renko and Machiko

Contents

Foreword

BETWEEN DECEMBER 7, 1941, AND THE END OF the Pacific war in 1945, Japan and the United States traded almost nothing but bullets, bombs, and bitter words. That changed abruptly on August 14, 1945. Japan, its cities and factories largely a bombed-out wasteland, accepted unconditional surrender, yielding its future to the tender mercies of the victorious Americans. A new era of trading was to begin.

Because of time differences, the day of surrender in Japan was August 15. I was sixteen years old, living with my brother-in-law in the outskirts of Tokyo. I was a middle school student and the following April I was to enroll in high school. But education took a backseat to national defense. Students my age were drafted to work in defense factories. My job was to assemble aircraft instruments.

On the day of surrender I was not at the factory because my brother-in-law told me there was no point in going to work. "I don't know what it is, but something very strange is going on," he said.

I remember listening at noon to the reedy, uncertain radio voice of Showa, the Japanese name for Emperor Hirohito, announcing the nation's capitulation. The stilted formal language the emperor used was difficult to understand, but I could tell that the war was over and Japan had lost. I remember little of that day other than that my lunch was a scanty bowl of rationed fried, defatted soybeans. Our area, surrounded by farmland, had escaped American aerial bombing, but not far distant were the ruins of what had been a metropolis. I remember a sense of relief rather than chagrin that we had lost the war.

The Japan of my youth, consisting principally of four mountainous islands with few resources, had lived by trading. It bought most of its raw materials abroad and converted them by ingenuity and hard work into goods that could be exchanged for more raw materials. In fact, it was the search for a cheap and reliable supply of critical resources that led to Japan's seizure of Manchuria in 1931 from a disorganized Chinese government. The United States, as a growing economic and political power, could not tolerate such lawlessness. Before long, Japan's continued military aggression and American determination to stop it escalated into the bloody Pacific war that ended with Tokyo's unconditional surrender.

Having devastated an implacable enemy, the United States then felt an obligation to strip Japan of any military capability while helping its erstwhile enemy to reshape itself into a democratic and peace-loving member of the family of nations. And in view of its lack of natural resources, Japan would have to support itself as a workshop, converting imported raw materials into products that could be sold abroad.

Ironically, Japan had been doing this ever since it entered the modern age after Commodore Matthew Perry, the American naval officer, persuaded feudal Japan to open its doors in 1853. How would the new industrial era differ from the old when most of its exports had been cheaply made novelties and consumer goods? Could Japan rebuild itself and survive by manufacturing and selling toys, lightbulbs, dinnerware, and cotton textiles produced by an immature industrial infrastructure, plus agricultural products like tea and raw silk? Hardly.

Even in defeat, Japanese industrialists in 1945 had more ambitious ideas for recovery. They would use their experience in the manufacture and fabrication of steel, shipbuilding, and other heavy industries and chemicals that had sustained their war effort, rebuild their country; and supply a vast Asian market.

Such an ambitious program would require capital, know-how, ingenuity, and even luck. (The recovery of one of the first segments of Japanese industry, ceramics, was stimulated by the demand for plumbing fixtures—Japan's sewage disposal system was primitive—at bases being constructed for American occupation forces.) Transportation facilities had been badly damaged by American bombs but people had to move around. Since private ownership of motor vehicles was virtually unknown, there was a big demand for bicycles. Companies like Honda hurried to meet the need. Before long, in addition to bicycles, Honda was manufacturing perky little motorcycles that found a ready market both domestically and in Southeast Asia and were embraced as a novelty in the United States. The Komatsu company converted its military tank production facilities to building bulldozers to level war-damaged buildings and reconstruct roads. A manufacturer of aircraft engine parts designed motorized irrigation pumps for Asia's endless rice fields. Laboratories that had developed radio communications equipment for Japan's armed forces renewed research into electronics, which led to inexpensive and popular pocket-sized radios.

Soon, however, that kind of rebuilding plan was discouraged by Joseph M. Dodge, the Detroit banker who was General Douglas MacArthur's economic adviser, and Edwin Pauley, the American directing the reparations program. Pauley made it known that the United States intended to seize industrial plants as reparations and perhaps move some of them to other parts of Asia devastated by the Japanese. And he quashed Japanese hopes of developing a market for sophisticated goods in the United States and Europe. Japan, he made clear, should look to recovery by focusing on the basic needs of the less developed countries of Asia. Japan's exports would be strictly regulated by a system of permits by GHQ.

The outbreak of the war in Korea in the summer of 1950 killed that strategy. Occupied Japan, still under U.S. rules, abruptly became not only a staging area for American forces sent to fight on the Asian mainland but also a supplier of almost everything other than ammunition that an army and a navy needed to fight a war. American purchases on the Japanese market—tank, Jeep, and truck repairs; aircraft and warship maintenance; fresh fruits and vegetables, R&R for recuperating troops—during the two and a half years of fighting in Korea are estimated at $2.3 billion. That is a sum that exceeds the direct reconstruction aid provided by the U.S. between 1945 and 1951.

The Japanese devoted a large part of the earnings from these sales to update and expand factories and facilities. Simultaneously, they improved their efficiency by adopting the quality control principles preached by an American engineer, W. Edwards Deming, who had been invited as a consultant. One of his strategies, quality control circles in which workers would meet regularly with supervisors to exchange views about ways of improving performance, was eagerly adopted because it reinforced the Japanese tradition of discussions leading to group decision-making. Deming is still revered in Japanese industrial circles. The annual Deming Prize for industrial excellence and innovation is still a prestigious national award.

The resurgence of Japanese industry was due in no small part to good planning as well as hard work. For example, most of Japan's postwar steel mills, incorporating the latest technology, were built on the shores of deepwater ports. Nearby shipyards used the steel to build not only giant supertankers but also huge dry-cargo freighters that would deliver coking coal from West Virginia and iron ore from Australia directly to the steel mills, with an important savings in handling costs. The aging American steel industry found it hard to compete.

After some expensive mistakes in designing consumer products for the American market, Japanese industry undertook extensive research. One notable example is Nissan, which, before entering the American market, shipped several of its cars to Los Angeles for testing. The engineers soon discovered that their vehicles lacked the power needed for accelerating nimbly onto high-speed freeways. And the boxy design, reminiscent of British taxis, held no appeal for Americans. So it was back to the drawing board.

The success Japanese car manufacturers have enjoyed in the American market is a tribute to the research that went into their design and engineering, In 1971, Japan produced 3.72 million passenger cars for the domestic and overseas markets and became the world's second largest builder. In 1975, Japanese motor vehicle exports to the U.S. reached 800,000 units, more than half of total American car imports, and Toyota replaced the German Volkswagen as the top import. Reliability and style were as important as price in penetrating the American market.

The steady progress of Japan as an industrial innovator is evident in the following chronology.

1950 Sony introduces its first home-produced tape recorder.

1953 Sharp begins sales of first home-produced black-and-white television set.

1955 Sony markets first home-produced transistor radios.

1960 Sony develops color TV sets and markets first portable TV receivers.

1966 Sharp introduced microwave ovens for home use.

1972 Casio markets electronic calculators.

1974 NEC introduces 16-bit microcomputer.

1977 Konika introduces first auto-focus cameras.

Japan's shift from labor-intensive products to technology-intensive goods, which inevitably were marketed worldwide, can be traced in the following timetable.

1950s	textiles
1960s	steel
First half of 1970s	TV sets
Latter half of 1970s	engineering machinery
First half of 1980s	automobiles, tape recorders
Latter half of 1980s	communication equipment, semi-conductors, computers

Pre-Korean War trade between the United States and Japan was, understandably, heavily lopsided. In 1947, the first postwar year in which Japan resumed foreign trade, Japanese exports to the United States amounted to only $30 million while imports from the United States were $460 million.

Japan was desperate to bring trade into balance as quickly as possible, and that led eventually to the semigovernmental Japan External Trade Organization (JETRO) to promote exports. Its strategy was to study the American market and introduce attractive Japanese products. By the time I joined JETRO in 1957, Japan's exports to the United States had risen to $600 million. But imports from the United States were $1.6 billion, resulting in an imbalance of approximately $1 billion.

It took nearly a decade to bring U.S.-Japanese trade closer to balancing. Japan enjoyed a surplus for the first time in 1965, amounting to $100 million. Since then, with the exception of

1967 and 1975, Japan has enjoyed a surplus largely thanks to products that improved year by year, and the ready acceptance in the American market of fine automobiles, television sets, computers, home tape recorders, and other electronic products requiring skilled engineering. It was my privilege to participate in a very small way in the campaign to promote these Japanese exports.

Parenthetically, I would like to note that although many believe the U.S. is virtually Japan's only customer, in actuality the United States is Japan's second best customer. Statistics for 2000, the latest available, show that 41.1 percent of Japan's exports were to Asia, while the U.S. share was 29.7 percent. The European Union lags at 16.3 percent.

In my later years with JETRO, there was an astonishing turn of events. JETRO's campaigning underwent a 180-degree change of course. Fearing further repercussions from the fast-growing trade imbalance, JETRO turned from advocating exports to promoting imports from the United States and other countries, and I was part of that campaign. The logic was that without a reasonable balance of trade, Japan would suffer costly consequences. And because Japanese manufacturers were doing an admirable job of selling abroad, JETRO directed its efforts to promoting imports. If U.S. cars were hard to sell in Japan because they consumed a lot of expensive gasoline and were too bulky for comfortable driving on the narrow highways, the Japanese would be persuaded to buy American fashions, cosmetics, kitchen ware, and even lumber cut to American dimensions for constructing spacious American-style homes. If imports of American oranges, apples, and cherries were opposed by Japanese growers, then it became JETRO's role to point out that there were luscious foreign varieties available before or after Japanese products hit the domestic market.

Remarkably, the reversal in policy was effected with minimal conflict, in large part because of general understanding, promoted by JETRO, that trade must be a two-way process.

This, then, is my story as a worker in the ranks of commerce, trying at first to introduce Japanese products to Americans, and then abruptly focusing my efforts on opening the Japanese market to American products. And since the story of trade is not all numbers, I have tried to tell that story in human terms rather than with the dry statistics of international commerce.

Preface

THE AVERAGE JAPANESE CERTAINLY KNOWS more about the United States than the average American knows about Japan.

What is the average American? That is impossible to determine. But if one were to stop ten Americans on the street of any city and ask them what they know about Japan, it is likely that none could tell you much more than that it is the country that attacked Pearl Harbor, that it now makes good automobiles, that the people eat with chopsticks, and that it has a mountain named something like "Fujiyammer."

By contrast, the average Japanese knows a great deal about the United States. He or she has learned through the media and during nine years of compulsory education (although virtually everyone completes twelve years) that the thirteen original colonies won independence from Great Britain in the Revolutionary War (the Japanese term is "War of Independence"); that there are now fifty states and that the country's leader is a president who is elected by the people and lives in the capital, Washington, D.C.; that there is a legislative body called Congress whose members are no wiser or reasonable than the men and women in the Japanese Diet; that the national language is English (a terribly difficult tongue); and that most Americans are wealthy although the country celebrate the New Year not solemnly and reverently as they do, but with a festival that features football games.

This knowledge may not be profound, but at least it is more extensive than the average American's knowledge of Japan. Alas, the information gap is widening. The Japanese media have perhaps as many as ten times the number of correspondents in the U.S. as American newspapers and television have in Japan. And the disparity in the number of tourists visiting the other country is perhaps ten to one in favor of Japan. Millions of Japanese now have access to the programs of the American Cable News Network as well as TV situation comedies with the dialogue dubbed in. Scores if not hundreds of American books are translated and published in Japan each year. In fact, Japanese publishers compete to buy translation rights to new American books but the reverse is not true. An American news magazine, *Newsweek*, publishes a Japanese- language edition simultaneously with its U.S. issue. And week after week the most exciting, if not the best, Hollywood movies are box-office hits in Japan.

Yet there is no greater understanding—I emphasize the word "understanding"—of America and Americans in Japan than of Japan in the United States. When Japanese find themselves beside an American in a Tokyo subway car, some feel uncomfortable enough to move to a different seat. One Japanese who had studied and worked in the U.S. and was supposedly an expert on America, recently told an American audience that in his view, ethnic diversity is at the root of U.S. weakness.

Oddly enough, the Japanese view of America tends to swing from one extreme to another. At one time, anything American was admired simply because it was American. The Japanese imported American music and business practices and adopted American social trends, fast food outlets, and fashions, particularly blue jeans. In the last decade, the tide has turned. Today some Japanese businessmen say they have nothing to learn from America, and in fact criticize American practices. It also should be noted that though at one time Japanese management styles were widely admired in U.S. business circles, that admiration evaporated when the Tokyo economy ran into problems.

Some Japanese see only the dark side of American society, viewing it as a land of gangs and crime where ordinary citizens carry pistols for their protection and drive-by shootings are routine. They criticize the U.S. race problems without seeing the progress America has made in advancing equal rights. They tend to ignore the persistence of discrimination in their own country against ethnic Koreans who have lived in Japan for several generations. Their disdain of American civilization spread a few years ago when a Japanese high school exchange student, Yoshi Hattori, was shot and killed in Louisiana when he approached a home in search of a Halloween party to which he had been invited. Widespread anger turned to loathing when the shooter was tried and acquitted.

Indeed, we people of the world's two most industrialized nations, so heavily dependent on each other, need to understand each other more clearly. It was with this need in mind that I decided to write this book.

How did I expect to achieve this objective? By sharing with readers in both countries the experiences and views developed over a lifetime of serving as a bridge between them. I was able to do this as an employee and executive of the Japan External Trade Organization (JETRO) for thirty-three years. For more than three decades I was involved closely, in one way or another, with U.S.-Japanese relations. My specialty was public relations, which must not be confused with trade promotion, which was JETRO's original mission. I lived and worked in the United States on two occasions: from 1962 to 1967 in New York City, and in Los Angeles from 1974 to 1977. As a JETRO official I visited America, as well as other parts of the world, scores of times on a wide variety of assignments, and hosted countless American missions to Japan. This responsibility enabled me to assess our guests frankly.

After retiring from JETRO in 1990, I moved to Denver, Colorado, and now consider it my home. It was from this base, in the American heartland, that I hoped to contribute to understanding between Americans and Japanese at the grassroots level.

My wife, Machiko, and I founded a small organization called Sogo Way as the vehicle for reaching our objective. Sogo Way published a monthly newsletter called *Understanding Japan*. It did not pretend to report the news, although the subjects it treated were linked, whenever possible, to current happenings. It was primarily an information letter about the Japanese, their customs, current interests and concerns, and the reasons for and historical origins of their way of life, which add up to their culture. Its goal was to promote understanding.

Sogo Way also published books. The first, titled *Old Man Thunder* and subtitled *Father of the Bullet Train,* is the life story of Shinji Sogo (my father, incidentally), the man responsible for creation of Japan's marvelous Shinkansen Bullet Train system. This present volume is one of several subsequent projects.

Machiko and I visited schools and conducted free seminars designed to promote understanding of the Japanese people. It was satisfying work, although "work" is hardly an appropriate word. Let me tell you, in the chapters that follow, how it all started and what I have learned from the experience.

Shinsaku Sogo
Denver, Colorado

Acknowledgements

IT'S CUSTOMARY FOR AMERICANS OF ACCOMPLISHMENT to credit their spouses for whatever success they may be enjoying. This is not always true in my native Japan where wives stay quietly in the background while their husbands bask in public attention.

My wife Machiko was that kind of woman, and at the same time she was not. She avoided attention for herself. But she prodded and pushed me to tell my story. Ultimately she made this book possible by, first, insisting that I set down my recollections in my native language, then spending endless hours making a rough translation into English for an American audience.

Long ago we had learned that a direct, literal translation of a Japanese manuscript does not necessarily make for interesting reading. So the next step was to ask our old friend, Bill Hosokawa, to help us. He had worked with us on our previous book, *Old Man Thunder: Father of the Bullet Train,* transforming our original manuscript into a story that has won much praise. He has performed the same kind of skilled rewriting and editing on this volume, transforming the manuscript into a book that deserves the catchy title, *From Foe to Friend: One Man's Experience in Japanese/American Trade.*

My only and deep regret is that Machiko, the "mother" of this book, is not here to enjoy its publication. But before cancer took her, she knew and was pleased that our book was on its way.

I dedicate it to her memory.

Shinsaku Sogo
Denver, Colorado

CHAPTER 1

An Innocent in New York

"YOUR TRANSFER TO OUR NEW YORK OFFICE," my boss said, leaning back in his chair, "will be approved officially at the board meeting this week. Prepare to serve there three years, perhaps four."

Surely he must be joking, I thought. Yet, nothing had changed since I heard the startling words. Outside the window the sky, as usual, was gray, the outline of nearby office buildings unimpressive. I was only a young employee in the Tokyo headquarters of JETRO, the semigovernmental Japan External Trade Organization, and only a few moments earlier had been summoned by the boss without a hint of warning. An overseas post was a dream job for a young Japanese bureaucrat, an assignment reserved for a promising few. I could not see the expression on my boss's face because I stood with head low, partly to demonstrate the required humility when summoned by a superior, partly to conceal my confusion.

"The director of Japan Trade Center's New York office," he went on, "has decided to assign you as assistant director of public relations. It is an important post. Make the most of it. Do your best for JETRO."

I bowed even lower.

The year was 1962. But even as I concealed my elation, which was the proper way for a Japanese junior official to act, I was aware of three huge problems standing in the way of meeting my agency's expectations: (1) My total American experience was a month in Chicago three years previously when my time was divided between a shabby hotel room and a drafty exhibition hall where Japanese products were on display. (2) My English was far from proficient. (3) I didn't have the vaguest idea what public relations was all about.

As a matter of fact, not many people anywhere in Japan had any extensive understanding of public relations. Few could say how it differed from sales promotion or advertising. As I learned later, the JETRO public relations division, established in 1958 shortly after JETRO became a government-subsidized organization, may have been the first in Japan. A history of JETRO suggests it is likely that an official who had heard of public relations in the United States thought it was a good idea and, when he came home, suggested an office be set up. JETRO liked the proposal and asked its parent organization, the Ministry of International Trade and Industry (MITI), to approve a public relations department.

MITI, the story goes, didn't know how to evaluate the request and asked the embassy in Washington to define the role of a PR department. The dictionary definition of public relations is simple: the business of inducing the public to have understanding for and goodwill toward a person, firm, or institution.

But there are additional questions: How is this accomplished? Isn't everything we do to promote our mission public relations? If this is so, what more must we do as public relations practitioners?

Someone on the embassy staff reported back that American companies hire public relations agents to manage their public relations activities. Employing experts to carry out the details seemed to be a reasonable strategy, and MITI went to the Ministry of Finance for funding. (Under the Japanese system, every government department has to appear at a Ministry of Finance hearing to justify its budget request.) Officials at the Finance Ministry were just as much in the dark as the other ministries, but this was in the good old days when bureaucrats were willing to give new ideas a try, so they approved funding.

If anyone in JETRO at the time understood public relations, the information had never reached my level. But who was I to question the decision to assign me to a public relations job? In fact, it was strange that I was working for JETRO at all. A series of unlikely circumstances had brought me to its offices.

After high school, I had the good fortune of being accepted by the elite Tokyo University. Most graduates of Tokyo University, at age twenty-two or twenty-three, went directly into government service or academia. I had wanted to work abroad, and at the time it appeared the best opportunity was in Brazil where the government was welcoming Japanese agricultural specialists. Thus I enrolled in the department of agriculture.

But when I was graduated in 1952, there were no offers of positions in Brazil. To support myself I did the unthinkable: I took a blue-collar job in the Tokyo plant of a rubber company where business was booming following the Korean War. My tenure there was short and uncomfortable. To be accepted by my fellow laborers it was necessary—and difficult—to conceal my family ties and university background. Before long I quit my job and joined the staff of a brother-in-law who was a member of the House of Councilors, the upper chamber of the national legislature, or Diet. Most such aides were, unlike me, ambitious to go into politics, and the staff jobs were an apprenticeship. I had no such interest.

One day, while flipping through an official report, I learned about a nonprofit organization that had been formed to promote exports by undertaking overseas market research. The organization was called JETRO. I hurried to apply for a position. In the summer of 1957 I was interviewed by JETRO's president, Teiichi Nagamura.

"All JETRO employees," he told me, "must be able to speak at least one foreign language. How about you?"

He was not entirely accurate about the linguistic ability of his staff, and neither was I completely candid when I said I could handle Portuguese. Regardless, I was hired. I was not the typical new employee. Most of them are taken on fresh out of college at twenty-two or twenty-three years of age. I was 28 and in my third job.

My work, though not particularly demanding, kept me at my desk quite late. Staying past regular office hours was standard in Japan at that time. Although there was always plenty of work to do, it was also customary to stretch the workload past the theoretical quitting time to provide the impression of great diligence. Nonetheless I enrolled in evening English-language classes at a school called the Japan-America Conversation Institute. It was run by Namiji Itabashi and his wife, both well-known and highly respected as English teachers. There were about twenty in my class: college students, businessmen, teachers, and even housewives, all highly motivated. The classes ran from 6 to 9 P.M. Because of the work at JETRO I seldom reached the school on time. On the occasions when there were genuine deadlines to be met at the office, it was nearly 9 o'clock when I dashed breathlessly into the classroom. Despite the sympathetic efforts of my teachers, I could not meet the requirements for graduation even after two years.

The history of JETRO reflects the evolution of Japan's trade policy after the end of World War II in 1945. A quickly stimulated export program was essential to rebuild the nation's war-devastated economy. The United States recognized this need, particularly with the growth of Soviet and Chinese Communist military power in the Far East. But a bit of typically Japanese psychology complicated matters.

For decades after the end of World war II, the Japanese could not get over the feeling that since they were the defeated and Americans were the victors, they should give in to whatever the U.S. demanded. After all, Japan had accepted "unconditional" surrender. The word "unconditional" was an adjective describing the nature of the surrender, but it permeated Japanese understanding of U.S.-Japanese relations for years.

It is likely that most Americans did not understand this Japanese feeling. After the peace treaty when the Occupation ended, it was the U.S. view that Japan no longer needed to be subservient, that the two nations should treat each other as equals. But from the widespread Japanese view, the victor was the victor and the loser the loser, and Japan could not say no to the U.S. It is probable that this mentality exists to some small extent even today.

What was the practical result of this psychology? While Japan was a defeated nation trying to regain its equilibrium, there was little friction in Japanese-U.S. trade relations. But when Japan began to show signs of a strong recovery and its exports became a powerful tool of that recovery, friction developed. The first important manifestation of that friction came early in 1956. Ten years after the end of the war, Japan's textile mills were turning out impressive quantities of cotton goods. They found excellent acceptance in the United States, much to the distress of American textile manufacturers in the Deep South. That resulted in pressure from Washington, which caused Japan to agree to "voluntary restraints" on the export of cotton goods.

Five years earlier, in 1951, about the time U.S. Secretary of State John Foster Dulles visited Japan to finalize terms of the peace treaty, JETRO was established in Osaka as the Japan Export Trade Research Organization (Zaidanhojin Kaigai Shijo Chosakai). Its mission was to research overseas marketing opportunities for Japanese products and publicize the findings among entrepreneurs. Great Britain had established the British Export Trade Research Organization

(BETRO) somewhat earlier, and there is good reason to believe Tokyo bureaucrats substituted the word "Japan" for "British" since the aims were similar. BETRO is no more, but JETRO thrives even though its mission was reversed, as we shall see.

In 1954 JETRO was merged with two private organizations to pursue four objectives: research overseas markets, organize trade fairs, promote trade, and conduct an advertising and publicity campaign for Japanese products. In 1958 JETRO became a semigovernmental agency whose budget and policy were controlled by MITI. A dozen years later JETRO's mission underwent a 180-degree change, promoting imports rather than exports. I will discuss this dramatic change later.

When I joined JETRO in 1957, it had twenty-one overseas offices. The oldest, at age three, was in New York. When I retired in 1990, there were seventy-six offices in fifty-seven countries, including seven in the United States.

Three months before I received my temporary Chicago assignment, JETRO had opened a one-man office there. When the Chicago International Trade Fair was scheduled, JETRO rented a booth to introduce Japanese products. But since the new JETRO office did not have the staff to take care of it, several of us from Tokyo, including an employee named Ippei Takeda, were sent to Chicago to take responsibility for the booth. The work involved unpacking and displaying goods loaned by Japanese manufacturers, manning the booth to answer visitor inquiries and see that nothing was stolen, and finally packing and returning the merchandise to the manufacturers. Nobody was giving away anything in those days except cheap paper fans. For both Takeda and me, it was the first overseas trip. We looked forward to it with great anticipation and not a little concern. The fact that friends and colleagues gave us *senbetsu*—traditional "farewell" money for a traveler who might not return from a hazardous trip—was not reassuring.

Japan Airlines at the time was still flying propeller planes across the vast Pacific. It was a long, exhausting flight to Honolulu, where we went through the confusion of U.S. immigration and customs inspection. Then there was another nine-hour hop to San Francisco where we were met by Shigeo Nagata from the local JETRO office.

What I remember best of my first view of America is the brilliant blue California sky and the white-painted houses—so different from the drab Japanese homes—climbing San Francisco's hills. Nagata-san took us to lunch. On the way out of the restaurant, Takeda handed our host some money, saying: "You left this on the table. I picked it up for you." In Japan a service charge, usually 10 percent, is added automatically to bills. We had learned about tipping.

A United Airlines jetliner sped us to Chicago over some incredibly desolate deserts, incredibly rugged mountains, and incredibly vast farmland. JETRO's man in Chicago, Takakiyo Ito, knowing of the agency's very limited budget, had reserved rooms for us at the Dearborn Plaza Hotel, which failed by far to live up to its imposing name. The monthly rent for each of us was $110. Where were the elegant American hotels we had seen in Hollywood movies? Takeda and I salved our disappointment by gorging on ice cream and frozen strawberries, a priceless treat in Japan, which we picked up in a nearby grocery store.

The trade fair was held in the old Navy Pier, which offered plenty of space but not much in the way of facilities. To get enough office space we had to rent a room at the Lakeshore Motel, which was within walking distance of the Navy Pier and offered amenities, including a swimming pool that we were too busy to use. We needed twenty attendants, preferably Japanese with business experience, for the 10,000-square-foot Japanese exhibit. Finding them proved to be impossible. The next choice was young Japanese who were studying in American schools and presumably fluent

A crowd of people waiting for the opening of the Chicago International Trade Fair (July 3–18, 1959). This was the first trade fair held in Chicago after the war. The fair was a huge success and drew such large crowds that the local fire squad had to restrict admittance.

in English. Only a few were available. Finally we settled for young Americans who were willing and enthusiastic but unfortunately knew next to nothing about Japan and Japanese products.

About twenty years later I happened to share the elevator in my Tokyo condo with an attractive young woman who, I learned, lived in the same building. She looked at me and then asked, "Aren't you the Mr. Sogo who hired me in Chicago?" Her name was Wakako Hironaka, and I remembered her as one of the few Japanese students who spoke English well. Now she is a member of the Diet and well-known as a translator. Among her books is a translation of Ezra Vogel's famous *Japan as No. 1*.

Today, Japanese exhibits at trade fairs are staffed by employees of the exhibitors familiar with their products. In Chicago we had to develop instant experts. When someone showed interest in an item, we grabbed a brochure and did the best we could.

Our attendants were paid weekly in cash. I am not sure why we didn't issue checks. Perhaps it was that checks were uncommon in Japan at the time and writing them was a bother. One day Takakiyo Ito took me to his bank and withdrew $3,000 in small bills, which he handed me. The money was to pay the attendants, with the balance to be placed in the office cash box.

I was extremely nervous about taking custody of so much cash. A quick calculation showed, to my consternation, that $3,000 was more than a million yen, or fifty-four times my monthly salary. If, somehow, I were to lose that money, I would be held personally responsible and the Japanese code of ethics would require that it be repaid. That would require my entire salary for four and a half years with no deductions for living expenses.

After glancing around the bank lobby to make sure no one was watching, I put the envelope holding the currency in the inside pocket of my jacket and hurried on foot, past a construction site, to the Lakeshore Motel. There seemed to be no one on the street, until suddenly a roughly dressed young man emerged from an alley and blocked my path. I tried to slip around him but he moved to cut me off. I had no alternative but to face him.

"I'm a sailor," he said, looking directly at me. "My ship left without me. I haven't had anything to eat. Give me a quarter."

Perhaps it was fright that enabled me to understand what he was saying. And I was too frightened to feel sorry for him. Quickly I asked myself what would happen if I gave him a quarter. Would he take me for a soft touch and ask for more? What if he demanded to see what was under the bulge in my jacket? Pretending I did not understand, I stared at him blankly.

The fellow took a step closer. Apparently realizing that I was a foreigner, he said loudly and slowly, "I am a sailor." He spelled out the word. S-A-I-L-O-R. "I not eat since yesterday. I have no money. No M-O-N-E-Y. Give me a quarter."

Of course I had a quarter. In fact, I had the equivalent of 12,000 quarters in my jacket. But I shook my head and, with sudden inspiration, replied in Japanese, "I am sorry, but I do not understand English."

The man who said he had no money for a meal took a quarter out of his pocket and held it before my face, "See," he said.

"This is a quarter and I'm telling you, give me a quarter."

I pretended to examine the coin and continued to feign ignorance. Suddenly a second man, also roughly dressed, popped out of the alley and approached us. "Hey, what's up?" he asked.

The first man whispered something in his ear. The second man began talking to me very slowly. "This man is a sailor," he said. "His ship left him, and he has eaten nothing since this morning. Give him a quarter."

Strangely, I felt no fear for myself, but I could think of nothing but to continue to play the part of the uncomprehending foreigner.

The two men whispered to each other, and suddenly one uttered an obscenity and said, "Let's go."

As soon as they were out of sight, my legs began to shake. I wanted to run but I could not move. A taxi came by and I flagged it down. "Lakeshore Motel," I gasped in a quaking voice. I could not stop trembling.

Back in the safety of the office, I regained enough composure to review my experience. I realized the sailor, if that's what he was, was simply panhandling. He wasn't armed and obviously didn't know I was carrying so much cash. I have no idea what would have happened if he knew I had a small fortune in my coat pocket. If something like that were to occur today, I am afraid I would be lucky not to be shot on the spot. I have never had a more frightening experience anywhere in the world.

The Chicago trade fair drew huge crowds. There was a pent-up demand for all kinds of goods, and throngs came to see what was available. In our booth were attractive new items such as transistor radios, 35 mm cameras and binoculars—a few of which were stolen until we learned to chain them to the tables—as well as more traditional goods like bottled soy sauce, chinaware, canned tuna, and mandarin oranges.

One day I discovered that all the attendants had left simultaneously on their lunch break, leaving me to man the booths alone. I had to answer visitors' questions while keeping an eye on others handling the cameras and testing the binoculars. While bouncing around in front of the displays I noticed a distinguished-looking, middle-aged man silently watching the scene. The next time I looked in his direction the man was gone, but soon he returned with a length of rope.

"Here," he said. "I'll tie one end to this post and you tie the other end to that post." The rope became a simple but effective barrier between the displays and the public, and suddenly my job was infinitely easier. Why hadn't I thought of that?

My look of gratitude must have moved him. "My name is Al Keller," he said. "How about lunch when your helpers come back?"

We went to one of the temporary eateries in the exhibition hall. There, over a simple meal, I learned his forebears were from Austria, that he was an engineer employed by General Motors in Columbus, Ohio, and that he was vacationing in Chicago. Somehow he made me feel warm and human. For a long time, in Japan and the United States, I had been engrossed in nothing but work. But Al's company brought me back in touch with the real me. As we chatted—he seemed to have no trouble understanding my halting English—I suddenly realized the day was my birthday. I thanked him for inviting me to lunch on my birthday.

Al Keller came by the booth a number of times after that, always asking, "Any more thefts? Let me know if you have any problems."

Being Japanese, I felt an obligation to return Al's kindness. I invited him to dinner in the dining room of a luxurious Dutch cruise liner that had tied up at the pier for the fair. We talked of many things. He asked what I would like to take home to Japan as a souvenir. American ballpoint pens and butane lighters were highly prized at the time, but I told him only that Japan had everything but large tracts of land.

On my birthday the following year I received a card and a $10 bill from Al. For several years after that, I would receive a card and $10. In 1962 when I was assigned to JETRO's New York office, Al invited me to the wedding of one of his seven adopted children. After my return to Japan, the birthday card and $10 bill were replaced by a telegram or a telephone call.

In 1990 I received a letter from Columbus, Ohio. It was from Marilyn Blake, who identified herself as Al Keller's niece. She had enclosed a newspaper clipping reporting Al's death and photographs taken at the cemetery. "He often spoke of you and your family," she wrote, "and I found your name and address among his files. I had been to see him at his apartment one month before he passed away and at the hospital three days before. I will miss him."

And so do I. Many years later I am still unsure what attracted us to each other. Perhaps he felt sorry for a naive, confused foreigner and was motivated by his inherent kindness, and I by the friendliness of a stranger in a strange land. Whatever the case, Al was my first American friend. Although we spent almost no time together, I had the utmost respect and affection for him. On my first visit to the United States my most lasting impression was not the vastness and wealth of the country, but the friendliness of an ordinary American named Al Keller.

My New York assignment began in February 1962. I had the title of assistant public relations director of the

Al Keller (back, center) was the first friend I made during my first visit to the United States. Our friendship lasted until his death in 1989. My wife and I were invited for the reception of his adopted daughter, and this photo was sent to me later. The following memo was attached to this photo: "To Mr. & Mrs. SOGO, A memorable day July 23, 1966 Kathleen & Bob wedding. 'No. 1 MAN' Al Keller."

JETRO office under Jiro Tokuyama, the director. But what were my duties? No one seemed able to explain what public relations consisted of. I gathered it was something between advertising and sales promotion, but I didn't know exactly what. To my great relief I discovered that an American firm, Ruder and Finn, had been retained to advise us and do most of the actual work. One of their account executives, Norman Weissman, came to the office almost daily and I asked him many questions.

On the day I arrived in New York, a commercial airliner had crashed with many fatalities. One of the victims was a JETRO employee. Early in our relationship I asked Weissman what advice he would have given the airline after the crash.

"I would advise the president to call a press conference as quickly as possible and provide all the information available—the number of victims, the circumstances of the crash, everything that's known about an unfortunate accident," Weissman said. "It's important to cooperate with the media in getting the facts out. I would also advise the company to cancel all advertising to let the public forget which particular airline was involved."

I learned two things from this conversation. First, when a serious problem arises, the most senior person in the organization should stand before the public and provide all the information available. Second, Americans do not apologize publicly for errors, real or imagined, the way Japanese do. They may say they're sorry, but from the Japanese point of view it lacks the sincerity, the depth of regret and remorse, involved in a Japanese apology.

Eijiro Fujise, president of the JETRO office in New York, told me an airline official had telephoned to inform him of the crash and death of the JETRO employee but, he fumed, "He never offered one word of apology."

I am sure the airline official said he was sorry to report the bad news, but in Fujise's mind that did not constitute a proper apology. A formal call on Fujise at his office, with much bowing and expressions of regret, would be the Japanese way. Even in America Japanese would expect such formality.

On the other hand, I learned over time that the way Japanese often say "*Sumimasen*," which can mean "I apologize" or "Excuse me," sounds insincere to many Americans and irritates them. "*Sumimasen*" is voiced so casually, automatically, and frequently that Americans may take it to be no more than an "oops," which acknowledges error but expresses no regret.

The difference between Japanese and American approaches to apology can be illustrated by another episode. One day we learned through the press that a shipment of transistor radios ordered from Japan by an American company contained nothing but rocks. This was a deplorable but isolated case of a particular Japanese firm cheating a customer, but it was a very distressing incident to a nation trying to establish its credibility. It moved Hajime Fukuda, then minister of International Trade and Industry, to offer a formal apology to the American firm.

Was the incident so serious that it required an apology by a cabinet minister? We discussed the matter in the New York JETRO office. Nothing was settled, of course, but it was pointed out that if the situation were reversed and an American firm had defrauded a Japanese firm, it was not likely the U.S. secretary of commerce would offer an apology in an incident involving two private companies. The Japanese government felt it was proper to apologize because it was afraid this private action reflected unfavorably on the entire nation, which many Japanese see as an extended family.

Apologies under any circumstance can be very sensitive. When the present emperor visited China for the first time, he is reported to have said, "I feel sorry for what happened between our two countries." That touched off a debate in Japan as to whether he was simply expressing his personal feelings. or was in reality apologizing for Japan's wartime aggression. He was free to do the former as an individual; the latter involved national policy, which was best left to the government. Although Japan and the U.S. have worked closely as trading partners and keepers of the peace in the Far East for more than a half century, national customs and fine cultural nuances relating to apologies still create friction and misunderstanding.

If I did not understand public relations, I learned one of its essences from Jiro Tokuyama, my New York boss and a person ahead of his time among Japanese. Unlike the representatives of most other Japanese enterprises in New York, he believed the essence of public relations was getting to know people. Almost daily he had lunch meetings with American journalists, business leaders, academics, and government officials at which he cultivated friendships and engaged in discussions about Japanese-American relationships. He accepted many invitations to speak and his English was good enough that he welcomed question-and-answer sessions. People got to know him and did not hesitate to contact him when they had a question or problem about Japan. His activities did not sit well with other Japanese in New York. He was thought to be too forward, too aggressive, lacking discretion and reserve, and was not appreciated by many of his colleagues and superiors in JETRO. But I was fortunate to come under his influence early in my career.

Because of my language inadequacies I went out of my way to avoid speaking engagements. Tokuyama changed that. He ordered me to take every opportunity to speak about Japan, particularly in high schools in the New York area.

"Think about it, Sogo," he said. "How many opportunities will you have in your lifetime to speak directly to an American audience about our country? Even the prime minister has only one opportunity a year when he visits the Foreign Correspondents' Club in Tokyo. Here, many groups want to hear what a Japanese has to say about Japan, even if your English may not be perfect."

After that, I went out at least once a week to speak to high school classes. At one school the teacher introducing me began: "Today we have a special guest speaker. He is..." Before she could finish, the teacher was interrupted by a boy in the back of the room shouting, "a Chinaman." I learned not to become flustered.

Another lesson I learned early on was the need for being prepared. American journalists want details. Generalities will not do. Soon after I arrived in New York, JETRO organized a handicrafts show to demonstrate the skills of traditional craftspeople. The objective was to combat the image of cheap and flimsy Japanese products. Jiro Tokuyama had me conduct a press briefing and it turned out to be a painful lesson.

"Of the 500 items on exhibit," one reporter asked, "which is the most expensive and which is the least expensive?"

I didn't have the slightest idea.

"What is the material in this piece? Is it cherry wood or oak?"

"Is new technology used in creating these traditional pieces?"

Mostly I had to stumble with the answers, promising to locate the information if it was important to the reporter. I quickly realized that we may have lost an opportunity to get some valuable publicity because I couldn't provide answers.

Early on, our JETRO office discovered that brochures and instructions accompanying Japanese goods often were printed in fractured English, unintelligible or so bad as to be ridiculous. There wasn't much that we could do for individual companies, usually small, except to urge them to seek competent help in preparing their materials.

Meanwhile, we set about to do whatever we could to improve English-language promotional materials. Some pamphlets and brochures could be edited, but others needed extensive rewriting. Tokyo demanded an estimate of cost. Our American consultants said it was impossible to provide an estimate until they actually began work, and that would cost money, too. I finally asked the Americans to give me an estimate of the time a particular job would take and their charge per hour.

This was a system Tokyo could understand. It may sound strange today, but Japanese at the time were spending large sums for tangible products such as a written report, yet they were reluctant to pay for something invisible such as a service or consultation. That is changing as Japanese become more aware of American practices.

American services are provided at an hourly rate, whether by blue-collar workers or professionals like lawyers. I learned that promptness is important and that the expression "Time is money" is a reflection of the real world. I think that is one reason why volunteer service for the benefit of others—a contribution of one's time—is so highly regarded in the United States.

Generally speaking, JETRO's program embraced two objectives. The first, but not necessarily most important, was to help market specific types of products. Various sources provided photographs and information and the hired PR people decided on the best way to use it in promotional campaigns.

The second and more important part was to improve the image of Japan and Japanese products in general, and thereby promote Japanese exports. We wanted to educate Americans about what kind of people the Japanese were, how they lived and worked, and how they designed and produced products that met world needs. The hired American PR people understood our objectives, but few of them knew anything about Japan. Little by little we educated them and they educated us, and the joint effort produced a series of five booklets that were educational and informative and that met our needs. Published in 1963, nearly two decades after the end of World War II, they were:

Quality Control in Japan reported Japan's success in designing and producing precision and high-tech goods and sought to correct the lingering image of cheap, shoddy products.

Industrial Design in Japan told of the originality and beauty of design in Japanese products and tried to overcome the impression that they were simply cheap copies of foreign products.

How Japan's Economy Works for You promoted the importance of cooperative trade relations between Japan and the United States.

Five kinds of booklets were published to improve the images of Japan and Japanese products. JETRO New York produced these with the help of PR consultants in 1963.

How Japanese People Live Today corrected the image of cheap Japanese labor living in houses of wood and paper.

How Japan Trade Center Serves You explains JETRO's function of promoting trade.

These titles today may sound dull and not of particular significance, but they were badly needed at the time. I would like to think they played a significant role in promoting understanding and bringing trade—which had been heavily in America's favor—into a more equitable balance. There is no point in reviewing the content of these booklets, but the story behind two of them may be interesting, partly because in a small way I was responsible for their publication.

Quality Control in Japan was, in effect, a tribute to Dr. Edward Deming, who had been invited to Japan by General Douglas MacArthur soon after the war's end to preach the gospel of quality control. He had traveled to many parts of Japan encouraging the business community to pick up the pieces and rebuild, with special emphasis on quality. One of his suggestions was for quality control circles in which the workers in a plant organized sessions to find ways of producing better products more efficiently. His ideas struck a responsive chord among Japanese, who do better in a group setting than as individuals. (The concept has not only survived, but grown. As of October 2000, according to a survey by the Japanese Institute of Science and Technology, there are 420,411 quality circles, with a membership of 3.2 million.)

The booklet's introduction was written by Dr. J. M. Juran, the editor of the *Quality Control* handbook. He wrote:

> It has been my privilege to observe quality control practice in a good many industries and countries around the world. To me, the striking factor about Japanese quality control has been the rate of progress. Prior to World War II, a ranking of industrialized countries, in terms of their quality of product, would have shown Japan at the foot of the ladder. In two short decades, Japanese industry has climbed that ladder rung by rung, until the nation has become generally competitive as to quality of product, and has reached a position of world leadership in some product categories. It is truly an outstanding achievement.

This was just the sort of endorsement needed by Japanese precision industries seeking markets for quality cameras, optical goods, ball bearings, timepieces, transistor radios, television receivers and broadcasting equipment, electronic calculators, and scientific and medical equipment. And just ahead was the bright new world of computers.

The booklet explained that Japanese products came under the scrutiny of the new Japanese Industrial Standards (JIS) law, and only those that passed rigid tests could carry the JIS label. I think it is safe to say that despite Dr. Deming's influence on American industry after his successes in Japan, he was mourned more widely in Japan than in the U.S. when he died in 1993.

Industrial Design in Japan was an effort to make it known that, although Japan had shamelessly copied foreign ideas in the past, it was now producing world-class industrial designers. The Tokyo University of the Arts had established the nation's first design major in 1951, and by 1963 there were ten universities offering design majors. Meanwhile, JETRO had added a design division to encourage improvements in the design of export items. One of its programs involved sponsoring a year of study abroad for "design interns." They were given a per diem allowance of $10, obviously not adequate but all that JETRO could afford, to see what was going on in their field around the world, and could even enroll in art and design schools. After their tours they were expected to visit various companies to preach the gospel of good design.

The purpose of this program requires explanation. It might seem at first glance that these young designers were being sent abroad to copy foreign designs. That was not the intent. The goal was to let them see the exciting things going on outside of Japan and inspire them to develop their own designs for the products that soon would be coming off assembly lines.

Unfortunately the program never became popular and soon was discontinued. The industrial design booklet outlined Japan's various intellectual-property protection laws, and how Japanese products had to meet standards established by the Japan Machine Design Center, the Japan General Merchandise Goods Export Design Center, and the requirements of the Ministry of International Trade and Industry. There is no way to know how many persons read the booklets and what good they did, but at least the information was made available, and often that is the only thing a public relations campaign can do.

The changing nature of Japanese industry and exports is evident in the products displayed at successive trade shows.

At the first U.S. World Trade Fair in 1957, the Japanese exhibit consisted primarily of carved wooden *kokeshi* dolls, iron kettles, lacquer trays, wooden and bamboo crafts, and chinaware, all beautifully crafted but reflecting an undeveloped economy. At the second World Trade Fair the following year, Japan wanted to present itself as an industrial nation but could only display large photographic panels with pictures of automobile factories, shipyards, steel mills, and power plants, plus one super-high-pressure insulator for power transmission lines. By the fifth Chicago International Trade Fair in 1963, four years after Ippei Takeda and I had supervised the JETRO booth, the Japanese exhibit included panels showing supertankers for transporting oil, high-speed trains, a parabolic antenna, a petrochemical plant, a nuclear-powered ship, a rocket, a commercial airliner, and an electric translation machine. Before long, Japanese exhibits at trade fairs around the world were showing portable color television receivers, computers, and robots that could handle large and heavy tasks or the finest kind of operation in the swiftly advancing science of electronics.

But it was not easy to overcome the impression that Japanese were copycats. Although Japanese exhibits were encouraged, sometimes it was difficult for Japanese visitors to wander at will through the exhibition halls because sponsors feared they would copy designs they saw. In one case a group of Japanese businessmen had the film in their cameras confiscated when they were seen photographing an exhibit. What secrets were there to steal from exhibits open to the public?

The World's Fair in New York in 1964 and 1965 became one of my major public relations responsibilities. The theme was "Peace Through Understanding," and the Japanese government, meaning JETRO and private industry, took over the Japan Pavilion.

Searching for the most effective way to carry out the theme, we came up with the idea of a "Teachers' Night," inviting several thousand high school teachers from New York, New Jersey, and Connecticut to a program at which we

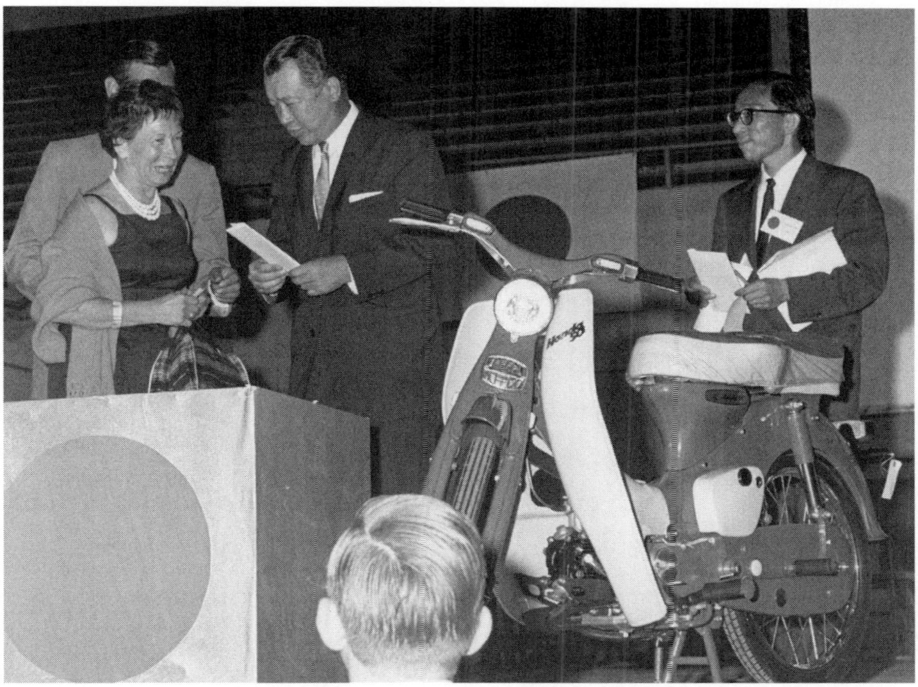

During this World's Fair in New York in 1964 and 1965, we celebrated Japan Day by organizing "Teachers' Night," a program appropriate to the theme of this exhibition (i.e., "Peace through Understanding"). Winning the first door prize, a Honda motorbike, the female teacher was very excited. The man in the middle, Kimitaka Murakami, was then-president of JETRO (June 28, 1965).

would expose them in a friendly way to information about Japan. But lacking funds, we had to do it as economically as possible. For the main feature we borrowed a film titled *Japan—A Profile of the Nation Today,* from the Japanese consulate general in New York. We also solicited door prizes from the now numerous Japanese firms

There was much more interest in Japan than we had anticipated. We had reserved a hall seating 3,000 but more than twice that many teachers sent in reservations. In desperation we had to ask each school to limit attendance to three teachers.

Learning from that experience, the Teachers Night for the following year was scheduled in an outdoor location seating 9,000. Then, fearful that perhaps our projection was too ambitious and the event would be marred by many empty seats, we added features to the program that we hoped would attract a crowd. We hired Sunny Fox, host of a popular TV program for children and well-known to teachers, as master of ceremonies. My boss, Jiro Tokuyama, prepared what I thought was an amusing and informative speech about the differences in Japanese and American customs. And we contracted with the New York Philharmonic with Keiko Kuyama, a Japanese woman then living in New York, as guest conductor. The concert was to feature the highly acclaimed Takashi Hironaka, playing Liszt's Piano Concerto.

As the day for the program approached, the weather forecast was not promising. If it rained, the entire program would have to be cancelled. Our contract with the Philharmonic was a modest $5,000, but it would have to be paid whether or not the performance was held, and at that exchange rate the $5,000 was the equivalent of ¥1.8 million, a staggering sum to justify in case it had to be spent for nothing.

As it turned out, the rain clouds disappeared. The music was beautiful. Sunny Fox did a fine job and Jiro Tokuyama scored a big hit. We received oodles of thank-you letters. But photos of me taken that night show a haggard little man looking close to total exhaustion.

These efforts may or may not have had an immediate effect on Japan's goal of selling more of its products in the United States, but I am confident they created goodwill, curiosity, and an open mind about Japan. And in time these developments were likely to help Japan's balance of payments, which then was running $4 to $5 million yearly in America's favor. Later the balance was to be reversed. But at the time I was in New York, we tried to get Americans to understand that in the previous decade Japan had bought almost $3 billion more from the U.S. than it had sold in return.

JETRO's main responsibility was to promote Japanese exports to bring that trade in better balance. Market research was still a large part of my duties, and I must confess it was not one of my favorite responsibilities. This is the way it worked: A Japanese manufacturer wishing to enter the American market would ask for a feasibility report. JETRO Tokyo would relay the request to JETRO New York. Since the report usually was on a specific product rather than an industry, the work was done under contract for the magnificent sum of $30. And because those of us in the New York office had regular assigned duties that kept us busy, contract reports (almost always needed very quickly) were not welcomed. In anticipation of such requests I had begun to keep a file of clippings about various products. One of the envelopes contained information about automobile seatbelts. I learned that New York, Wisconsin, and Virginia were considering making seatbelts mandatory, and if such a law were adopted nationwide, there would be some 60 million cars on the streets requiring belts in addition to all the new cars coming off the assembly line. I wrote an item that Tsuneharu Someya, head of the research department, included in his Friday report to

My boss, Jiro Tokuyama (right), director of public relations, JETRO New York. Successfully closing the Japan Day program, we felt relieved (June 28, 1965).

Tokyo. A month later I received orders for a contract report asking for a list of all seat belt and buckle manufacturers in the United States, their production volume, whether they manufactured belts or simply assembled them, and so on. Soon, three more Japanese companies asked for similar information. I am not sure what happened as a result of my reports, but it was reassuring that JETRO's publications were being noticed.

In December 1966, after nearly five years in New York, I was rotated back to Tokyo for a new assignment. I had learned a great deal about public relations but I was still far from being able to say I understood its fine nuances. And I was aware of two shortcomings in my experience: I had never been able to become part of the New York community, whatever that might mean. And although I had a number of American associates, I had made no friends other than my contact at long distance with Al Keller.

Chapter 2

Inside JETRO

I had no illusions about my public relations skills when I returned to Tokyo but my new assignment was a shock. I was named assistant director of the Personnel Division in the General Affairs Department, a long title for a not particularly significant housekeeping assignment. The Japanese management system creates generalists who are given responsibilities in a variety of functions. The American system is to develop specialists, such as sales or budgeting or advertising. I felt that what I had learned about public relations during my New York assignment was being completely wasted as I spent my time calculating salary adjustments, organizing staff training, and seeing off employees going abroad and welcoming those returning from overseas assignments.

My training lectures seemed to make an impression on the new employees, but some years later one of them told me what he remembered best of those sessions was the way I parted my hair. "Seventy percent on one side, 30 percent on the other," he said. I wear my hair the same way today, but there is much less of it.

No one in my first classes for new employees had traveled abroad or lived abroad because of a parent's overseas assignment. Today a large percentage of new employees have lived abroad or gone to school abroad, reflecting the greater internationalization of Japanese business.

The Personnel Division director sensed my dissatisfaction with my responsibilities and put me in charge of staff training. The practice then was to start by giving new employees—hired straight out of college in April—a one-week indoctrination course, after which they would be assigned to various divisions for on-the-job training. My big boss instructed me to extend the orientation course to a month, including much material on JETRO's purpose and goals in addition to the mechanical details about the organization. It had been the custom for the directors of various divisions and departments to address new employees about their responsibilities, but the program hadn't been working out. Directors, as part of their function, were out late almost every night working or entertaining overseas visitors, and as a result they frequently failed to get to the office by the scheduled 9:30 A.M. start of their lectures, which they liked to get out of the way before attending to their other duties. The impression this left on the new employees was not good. I changed the schedule, using the first half hour of each day to talk of my experiences in New York and air my own thoughts about JETRO's mission. Sometimes I would bring a complete Sunday edition of the *New York Times*, huge compared to the Japanese newspapers, to illustrate points I wanted to make about news coverage, advertising and editorial opinion, and important differences between the two countries.

I am not sure of the reason, but within eighteen months, a relatively short tour of duty, I was transferred from personnel to director of the PR Division in the Overseas Activities Department. The date was July 1, 1968. It was just the kind of assignment I had been hoping for. I now had the opportunity and authority to put to work some of the lessons I had learned in New York. But first there was another great hurdle to overcome.

Within a few days of my appointment, I was scheduled to appear before a panel of five MITI officials to justify my PR Division's budget for the coming year. The annual budget justification process is a major headache because every little item must be explained to officials who often have no idea what is involved. Since JETRO came under the jurisdiction of MITI, our budget request had to be approved by a MITI committee before being forwarded to the Ministry of Finance for final approval. In my case the difficulty was multiplied by the fact that I had had no input in drawing up the overseas public relations budget. On top of it all, I soon discovered the MITI officials had virtually no idea what public relations involved.

The budget hearing, conducted by five stern-looking MITI officials, was held in a JETRO conference room. The MITI group was headed by Michiro Uga, a man with a deep voice and a round face that never displayed emotion. The first of the JETRO people called was Yoshio Yano, director of the Activities Management Division of the Overseas Activities Department.

Yano was behind closed doors with Uga and his board almost nonstop from 9 A.M. to 5 P.M. while I waited outside in the large room where other departmental employees worked. When he finally emerged, Yano's face was flushed. While his people waited expectantly, he said, "Go home. All of you. You do not have to work any more today."

Then it was my turn to face Uga and the board.

As I took my seat Uga, without preliminaries said, "The budget for production of overseas PR films will be cut in half."

I was familiar enough with past budgets to know that these films were quite effective, and appropriations for six films annually had won routine approval. I started to speak but Uga cut me off. He went down the budget item by item, curtly ordering each proposal for increase cut in half or rejected altogether. All the while, he rumbled on about the foolishness of JETRO's public relations program, calling it a waste of taxpayer money. The other members of the MITI board nodded in approval. As Uga went on with his criticism of JETRO, the faces of my New York colleagues flashed before my eyes. No day was too long, no assignment too trying, as they worked to promote Japan and Japanese products. And here was this stupid Uga, ignorant of our efforts, heedless of what JETRO employees were trying to do, arbitrarily slashing the funds needed to carry out their duties.

"This next request is denied," I heard Uga say.

"Fine," I replied loudly without trying to conceal my anger.

Uga looked at me sharply. "If you want further explanation, have your executive director get in touch with me." My hearing was over in fifteen minutes.

I suppose the MITI people thought they were performing their duty by limiting spending, but arbitrary budget cuts without understanding JETRO's goals and strategy for achieving them were damaging to the national effort. To have our plans thrown back in our faces was demoralizing.

Hideo Kumeda, a high MITI official on temporary assignment to JETRO, summoned me for a scolding. "I understand that you caved in at your budget hearing," he said. "You must not allow that to happen again. You must fight as hard as you can to protect our interests. You should be aware that much thought, many discussions and compromises, within this organization have gone into budget planning, and the request JETRO makes to MITI must be defended at all costs if we are to function properly. If a newly appointed division director like you does not fight to the utmost to protect his budget, it can cause serious repercussions within JETRO."

I understood what he was saying, but I did not understand what I, a junior official new to his job, could do to resist a senior official's bullying. I said the equivalent of "Yes, sir" to Kumeda and promised to do better. I was never comfortable with money matters and I never became good at budget negotiations. In fact I regarded the entire budgeting process as something of a farce. July and August were the time for preparing the next budget and almost all other work stopped while budget discussions were held, often late into the night. Then the hearings, such as the one in which I failed to distinguish myself, were held, after which each ministry submitted its recommendations to the Ministry of Finance.

Sometime in December, the Ministry of Finance would announce details of the following year's budget. There was no scheduled time of announcement, but the information was of such great interest that many government employees stayed at their desks late at night to be on hand if the information should be released. Almost invariably the announcements were made between midnight and 6 A.M., almost never during regular working hours. I do not know the reason for this practice, unless it is the Ministry of Finance's way of demonstrating its importance.

Many if not most of the appropriations were expected to be inadequate. In anticipation, the various agencies were ready with a revised or amended request to be filed as quickly as possible. All this was a huge waste of time and energy. I am sure that this silly process cost the taxpayer more than was saved by the Finance Ministry's illogical parsimony.

As for my department, I decided it made more sense to work on international public relations indirectly, that is, by improving domestic public relations activities. I reasoned that if my department could demonstrate the value of promoting public relations within the country, JETRO would face less resistance from the bureaucracy in expanding overseas programs. That strategy was to work better than I had dreamed possible.

But to begin with this was, to coin a phrase, easier said than done because of the extremely rigid walls separating the domains of the various departments. We ran into the barriers almost immediately. When I suggested that it might be useful if employees of my PR Division contributed items to *JETRO Daily* (*Tsusho Koho*) and the monthly *Overseas Market* (*Kaigai Shijo*), I was reminded firmly that only personnel from the Research Department were permitted to write for these publications.

I should have known about this sectionalism from my experience in New York. There, Tsuneharu Someya, director of the JETRO office's Research Department, each Friday sent a news story called "New York Report" to Tokyo for publication in *JETRO Daily*. Someya encouraged others in the office, whatever their primary responsibility, to be on the lookout for interesting or useful items that could be sent to Tokyo as part of his report. My item on the seatbelts had been one of them. It wasn't that Someya wanted to take the credit for a comprehensive report; he was experienced enough to know that items sent by employees in other departments would not be printed.

On another occasion I had written a detailed report titled "How We Can Sell More Japanese Cars in the U.S." based in part on analysis of the very successful Volkswagen strategy. Since it was too long to be included in the "New York Report," I sent it directly to Tokyo. For a long time I heard nothing. I had all but forgotten about the report when it appeared as a three-part article in *JETRO Daily*. I was more puzzled than pleased. Later, I learned the problem had been with neither the length nor the contents of the article, but with the fact that it had not been sent from the Research Department. Ultimately, the New York PR Department had exerted enough pressure in Tokyo to bring about publication of what it considered to be a valuable document.

I believe this strict compartmentalization—perhaps "sectionalism" is a better word—which seems to be a part of Japanese business life, is largely responsible for the complaints of foreign businessmen that the Japanese market is closed or at least rigidly restricted. I can sympathize with their frustration with a bureaucracy that seems to be dedicated to delaying, rather than expediting, business. It is not only the system but also people's attitude in implementation of the laws that makes Japan's market seem more restricted than it actually is. Japan must overcome this infectious sectionalism. In addition to removing restrictive red tape, Japan must open people's minds and eliminate artificial barriers.

In seeking a broader role for my PR Division, I went one day to see Masao Okamoto, one of two division chiefs in the powerful Research Department, to propose that an entire issue of *Overseas Market* be devoted to the subject of public relations. It was a wild idea for which I did not hold much hope. But his answer stunned me.

"Sure," he said "How about the February issue?"

That was the very next issue. I had expected arguments as to why it could not be done. Sometime later I learned why he had been so accommodating. His staff was deep in preparation of a comprehensive White Paper on overseas markets and he was happy to give another department temporary responsibility for the magazine. By chance, my scheme for working on international public relations by emphasizing domestic public relations was becoming reality.

The theme for the issue had been set as "Public Relations: What Should We Do Overseas?" But as editor, I did not seek to answer the question. Instead I selected articles with titles like "How Japan and Japanese Products Are Evaluated Overseas and What the Criticisms Are." This article was based on a survey taken at the Ohio State Fair.

Another article was titled, "What Japan Can Do to Establish and Maintain Trust Towards Japan and Japanese Products." Each section cited specific examples provided by JETRO offices abroad—the U.S., Canada, Australia, Western and Eastern Europe, Southeast Asia, South America, North Africa, and the Middle East.

The issue was the largest to date for *Overseas Market*. We paid for the extra cost of paper and printing by selling advertising. We also set a precedent by illustrating the articles with photographs to brighten the magazine's appearance. This made it look like a magazine rather than a dull official report.

And then we used a PR strategy I had learned in New York: we prepared a three-page news release about the issue and distributed copies to newspaper and television reporters covering JETRO and trade issues. This news release informed lazy reporters of what they could expect to find in the issue and saved the time of the good reporters, thus improving our chances of being noticed. When the February *Overseas Market* was released the next day, we received extensive coverage in the press and on TV. People read these news stories, obtained copies of *Overseas Market,* and talked about the articles. What we had accomplished was the essence of public relations: capture the attention of the public through publicity, then hit them with the message. This was something that even some members of our PR Division had not understood. It was rewarding to see them come to the realization of what a PR campaign could achieve.

There is a fine line between advertising, sales promotion, and public relations activity. Each supports the others and sometimes their functions overlap. Advertising and sales promotion are designed to bring a product to public attention with the intention of getting buyers to buy it. The cash register measures the degree of success. On the other hand, public relations focuses on helping the public to understand a product, a company, a service, an issue, or even a nation's position. Public relations cannot accomplish its goals as if by magic; it is a science that sheds light on whatever it is that needs to be noticed and draws public attention—hopefully favorable—to specific issues or things. After that, the subject of this attention must stand on its own merits.

The issue of *Overseas Market* also carried a warning that was to be heard many times in the future, reflecting Americans' increasing frustration with what was perceived as a one-sided flood of Japanese products reaching the American market. This in essence is what it said:

> Japan's exports to the United States have been increasing rapidly, and various Japanese consumer goods from sandals to automobiles are pouring into the U.S. market. On the other hand, Japan has been creating the perception that it will not open its market to American products. Americans increasingly view this as unfair, and therefore the American view of Japan is not as favorable as before. Furthermore, Japan does not contribute to the stability of world politics and economy as much as it should in view of the fact that it has become the world's third largest industrial economy. Japan's trade relationship with the U.S. is one-sided.

Although the United States in the immediate postwar years had enjoyed a very substantial advantage in the balance of trade with Japan, the fact that Japanese sales to America had just about achieved parity was worrying Americans. Increasingly, Japan was described in the American media as an "economic animal" intent on "economic invasion" of the world's markets.

Of course the situation has changed greatly since 1969, but Japan's trade surplus has continued to increase despite strenuous efforts on both sides. In fact, on several occasions Japan "voluntarily" limited export to the United States of such items as color TV sets, textiles, and steel in response to American complaints. These concessions enjoyed only limited success. I will explore these developments in greater detail in another chapter.

In recent years Japan has taken a very substantial role in the world as a member of the United Nations, sending troops on peacekeeping missions to places like Cambodia and Mozambique, on minesweeping assignments after the Gulf War, and exceeding even the generous Americans in the amount of monetary and medical aid provided to needy countries around the world. The Japanese have been accused of prospering under the protection of the America defense umbrella, but the reality is that Japan pays virtually the entire cost—other than salaries—of maintaining U.S. forces on its territory. Unfortunately, little of this is known to Americans, which may be considered a failure of Japan's overall public relations program.

In the short term, however, many Japanese seemed to become aware for the first time what we in JETRO were trying to do other than sell Japanese products. I appeared on television programs, was invited to speak to various groups, and was interviewed by newspapers. On every possible occasion I tried to explain what JETRO's public relations program was all about. And *Overseas Market* was given a new mission: each February issue was devoted to a public relations theme.

In 1970 we tried to educate Japanese readers about how the world viewed Japan. It must have made for eye-opening reading, which I will share in a later chapter.

JETRO PUBLISHED THE MONTHLY MAGAZINE *OVERSEAS MARKET*. EVERY YEAR ITS FEBRUARY ISSUE WAS A SPECIAL PR EDITION TO PROMOTE PUBLIC RELATIONS, WHICH WAS THEN AN UNFAMILIAR CONCEPT FOR THE JAPANESE.

The theme in 1971 was building a corporate image for Japanese firms overseas. It featured the views of a number of Americans, including a journalist, young executives from shipping and electric companies, an international lawyer, a banker, and an airline official. The gist of their remarks was that they felt no hostility toward the Japanese people, but were frustrated that Japan seemed reluctant to take significant action to minimize trade barriers. "Japan should shoulder its fair share of the burden of improving the world economy," one wrote.

If that didn't catch the attention of our readers, President Richard Nixon did. On August 15, 1971, he announced an eight-point policy to protect the dollar, including suspension of the gold standard and a "temporary" 10 percent levy on imports. Nixon was reported to be unhappy with the way negotiations were going on reversion of Okinawa to Japanese control and on imports of Japanese textiles. The Japanese did not miss the significance of the date, August 15.

It was the anniversary of Japan's surrender that ended World War II.

CHAPTER 3

"Made in Japan"

JETRO's ORIGINAL MISSION WAS to promote sale of Japanese products in overseas markets, and we never lost sight of it even as the agency was seeking to build up two-way trade by increasing imports. The logic, of course, was that Japan could not buy from other nations unless it exported its own products. And it was essential to understand the market if Japan was to do a good job of selling. Therefore, JETRO conducted several surveys to help Japanese producers understand the market.

In the summer of 1966, JETRO asked a number of visitors at the Washington State Fair what items they thought of when they saw a "Made in Japan" label. The most frequently mentioned were cameras, silk, and motorcycles. Two years later a survey at the Ohio State Fair listed cameras, toys, electronic equipment, and motorcycles.

At about the same time, a wide-ranging random survey of both average consumers and so-called opinion leaders was taken in various American communities about their perception of the quality of Japanese goods. There was little difference between the responses of the two groups. It was encouraging to find only 5 percent of average consumers and 13 percent of opinion leaders thought Japanese products were still cheap and of low quality. That dubious honor was being taken over by other Asian nations just entering the industrial age, which made it all the more important for Japan to emphasize quality in its products. MITI launched a campaign to promote the idea that "Made in Japan" was a guarantee of superior design and workmanship, and JETRO was assigned the public relations role. But first we had to know what consumers were thinking, and why.

In 1967–1968 JETRO surveyed 100 women consumers in Chicago about their preferences in dinnerware. They were shown products made in Japan, the United States, Norway, West Germany, and Sweden. Fifty of the women were told the country of origin for each product, the other fifty were not. The answers were confusing. The informed group tended to rate Japanese products lower in terms of quality and price. But when all the women were asked whether their evaluation was affected by knowing a product was made in Japan, 75 percent said they saw no connection between country of origin and quality. However, one person said the fact that the product was made in Japan increased its value, while ten said they believed Japanese products were inferior. Perhaps the sampling had been too small for the findings to be meaningful.

In the immediate postwar decades, tableware had been an important export item. For some reason most of it was manufactured in Tsubame City in Niigata Prefecture on the

Japan Sea side of Honshu. However, with wages rising in Japan and increasing competition from other Asian nations, exports had been slumping. MITI picked tableware for special promotion and again JETRO was assigned to handle the public relations.

The overall strategy was based on the success of the German Solingen brand, known worldwide for the high quality of its cutlery. Most people thought Solingen was the name of the manufacturer. In reality there are a number of manufacturers that are allowed to market under the Solingen name if they meet a uniformly high standard. The decision in Japan was to upgrade its tableware by uniting leading manufactures under the unified Tsubame brand name and marketing an especially high-quality product. I was still in New York at the time and worked on the promotion with our consultant, Norman Weissman.

We prepared an elegant showroom, spotlighting gleaming silver in beautiful table settings. Weissman's agency produced a press kit with a dark blue velvet cover displaying a silver Tsubame logo. When I commented on the very substantial cost, Weissman explained: "We want to project the impression that Tsubame is the world's finest in tableware regardless of the country of origin. Everything we do should be designed with that in mind. Take a look at Cadillac's brochure."

I got the idea. The Chicago survey had shown that even with a product as uncomplicated as tableware, the old image of Japanese goods remained. As in the dinnerware survey, Japanese products received high marks when the country of origin was not made known, But when the women in the survey were told where the tableware had been manufactured, they were less enthusiastic about it. There was much to be done to improve image as well as improve product.

As part of the campaign to publicize the Tsubame project, Jack McDermott, a writer for *Gift and Tableware Reporter,* and Earl Lifshey, editor of *Home Furnishings Daily,* were invited to Japan at our expense to tour manufacturing plants at Tsubame City and, not incidentally, to be entertained and familiarized with Japan. It was clearly understood that these visitors could see whatever they wanted to see, talk to whomever they wanted to talk to, write whatever they wanted to write. These, of course, were and are standard procedures for helping the media, whose resources are usually limited, to produce the kind of publicity sponsors hope they will produce. And what our friends experienced must have been enlightening because their stories were more favorable than we had hoped for.

Even so, the campaign was doomed from the beginning for reasons not directly related to consumer preferences. In concentrating on public perceptions, we had neglected our public relations with two very important segments of the industry—the manufacturers and the marketers.

Some manufacturers complained that Tsubame standards were set too high; that some companies with outdated technology could not meet the new requirements, could not afford to install new equipment, and would go out of business. They contended that any government-supported marketing program should not discriminate against particular companies. Their complaints were heeded even though the effect was to lower standards and defeat the purpose of the Tsubame campaign.

American marketers also complained. Both importers and retailers liked the idea of a unified mark, but argued that they had spent liberally to promote particular Japanese brand names and that introduction of a new unified name—about which they had not been consulted—would only undermine their own efforts without a large, prolonged and expensive publicity and advertising program.

Who could pronounce Tsubame? For a Japanese it's easy: *tsu bah meh*. But for Americans it was likely to come out something like *tasu bame*. The Tsubame campaign was soon aborted. We had learned painfully the importance of touching base with everyone concerned, although this is something we should have known. The Japanese system of decision-making, called *nemawashi,* is a slow, low-pressure process that eventually brings everyone aboard. The expression comes from the technique of gently digging out the roots of a tree a little at a time to avoid shock, so that eventually it can be transplanted successfully. We had neglected to mind our own public relations in our enthusiasm to get the Tsubame project under way.

We had much greater success with a product not commonly associated with Japan: woolen fabrics. In the 1960s one suit of every three worn by American men was tailored in the United States from wool processed in Japan. The fabric was of good quality and relatively inexpensive, but the manufacturers were reluctant to disclose the origin for fear of driving down prices. By 1968, however, with the United

States hinting about import restrictions for Japanese textiles, a public relations campaign was under consideration. There were arguments pro and con.

Those who opposed the PR campaign saw no reason to promote Japanese woolens during a general trade dispute. They pointed out that Japanese woolens made up more than 70 percent of U.S. textile imports and that further promotion was unnecessary. Besides, they said, it was difficult to promote bolts of unidentifiable textiles that had yet to be processed into a final consumer product.

On the other hand, those supporting a campaign cited the need not to sell more product but to improve the image of Japanese wool. And it was more important, they argued, to establish an identity before the United States carried out its threat to require all imported material to bear the name of the country of origin. If Japan was producing and selling a superior product, why be reluctant to acknowledge the fact? Unlike the experience with Tsubame tableware, Japanese exported woolen fabric was of uniformly high quality, and we would be promoting a product rather than a particular brand name.

When the decision was made to go ahead, an agency named the Japan Woolen Information Council (JWIC) was set up in New York. Among its projects was a slickly produced booklet titled "Think Fashion, Think Fabric," which extolled the virtues of Japanese woolens and was widely distributed.

To further promote awareness of Japanese woolens, writers for publications like *Gentleman's Quarterly* and

Menswear were invited to Japan to visit factories and meet fabric and fashion designers. Everett Mattlin of the Quarterly also was a syndicated columnist, and his comments about the high quality of Japanese woolens appeared in a number of leading U.S. newspapers.

All of this was a great learning experience for me, particularly the proposal from our consultants in New York to invite Bill Blass to Japan. I had never heard of him, but agreed to accept the suggestion. He was given a tour, which he enjoyed very much, and when we learned how important he was in the world of American fashion design, we lost no time in persuading him to cooperate in producing a brochure titled "Bill Blass Talks Menswear." We also produced a three-minute TV clip with the same title for widespread distribution.

However, the most memorable event in the woolen textiles PR campaign was a two-week exhibit titled "East Meets West Fortnight" in the fall of 1969 at the Neiman Marcus flagship store in Dallas. At the opening reception President Stanley Marcus declared: "The men's suits exhibited here are made from the highest quality Japanese woolen textiles. Since World War II, through the efforts of their industry, Japanese woolen materials have greatly improved.... Japanese textiles in general and woolen materials in particular are excellent products, just like the Japanese television sets you see here. It is unfortunate that they are not widely known. Neiman Marcus will be expanding its Japanese products in the future."

I was ecstatic. No one had suggested to Stanley Marcus what he should say. No publicity person had written his speech. He had picked his own theme based on his own experience, and that is the best kind of endorsement. What more could a PR practitioner expect?

The woolen fabrics campaign had been projected for three years. It is difficult to assess its success, but I was very pleased with the way the campaign had been executed. We had brought the attention of American consumers to the fact that Japan was producing excellent woolen textiles in addition to cameras and TV sets. Unlike the Tsubame campaign, this one had been well planned and well executed. We were learning.

On the other hand, the wool campaign turned out to be a case of winning the battle but losing the war. Japanese export of cotton textiles was a much larger issue that, because of domestic implications on both sides, cast a shadow over Japanese-U.S. relations for a decade and a half.

In 1956, which was two years before JETRO was founded, the U.S. pressed on Japan what was called a voluntary restraint agreement on export of cotton goods. But the issue kept coming up and became particularly important in the U.S. presidential campaign of 1968 when Richard Nixon ran against Hubert Humphrey. Winning the South with its strong cotton and textile industries was critical for Nixon's hopes. He made protection of textiles a part of his campaign. And an agreement on textiles became linked with the negotiations to return Okinawa to Japan.

Japan and the United States agreed on terms of the reversion of Okinawa in late 1969, but six months later, negotiations on textile exports broke down. A textiles pact was not reached until January 1972.

Viewed in the long light of history, the textile disagreement becomes a case of intensely serious psychological shadowboxing in postwar U.S.-Japanese trade relations to which JETRO was a largely inactive bystander. Let me try to analyze it.

After the end of World War II, the Japanese were deeply aware that they had been defeated and the United States was the "unconditional" victor. "Unconditional" became the inevitable adjective preceding "surrender" in the Japanese media and Japanese psychology, and this was reflected in Japanese relations with and outlook toward the United States. It is likely that Americans did not share this victor-vanquished psychology. After all, the war had been fought, the Japanese defeated, and it was time to go on with no need for a peaceful Japan to be subservient to the U.S.

But for many Japanese a winner was the winner; the loser was the loser and had to abide by the winner's demands. Thus Japan could not say no to the U.S., and some of that mentality remains even today. Perhaps this is a psychological remnant from feudal Japan when the victor in battle showed little mercy and the vanquished often chose suicide. As trade issues intensified, in each case it was the United States that pushed and Japan that yielded. Off the record, American negotiators indicated it was their strategy to push and push and push because in the end Japan would never say no.

But Japan did say no in 1970 when the textile talks broke down. It was newsworthy enough in Japan for the mass-circulation *Yomiuri Shimbun* to report the story under a headline that read "For the First Time After WWII, Japan Says 'No' to U.S."

Despite a series of concessions, Japan's trade balance continued to grow. In 1965, Japan showed a trade surplus for the first time after World War II. That surplus was a modest $283 million, but since then, Japan's continued to grow each year except in 1967 and 1968. But the trend was obvious; in 1971 Japan's exports increased by 24.3 percent over the previous year.

This was not enough to give Japan a sense of security. Japan was aware of the fragility of its economy and fearful that the good times would not last. These fears were confirmed when soaring oil prices reversed the trade balance sharply in 1973, 1974 and 1975.

But the U.S. did not change its tactics of demanding restraints. When Japan complained that the Americans were not trying hard enough to enlarge their Japanese market, the U.S. cited what it called "a variety of visible and invisible barriers" that discouraged sales. I watched with alarm as expressions such as *hanbei* (anti-American), *kenbei* (hatred of America), and *bubei* (insulting American) appeared more frequently in the daily press.

In 1989, Shintaro Ishihara, a leading commentator and now governor of Tokyo, together with Akio Morita, the late chairman of the Sony group, published a book titled *The Japan That Could Say No*. It created quite a stir in both the United States and Japan. Many considered it a kind of economic declaration of independence in which Japan was asserting its maturity.

When Japan was a developing nation recovering from the war, there was no trade friction with the United States.

Japan's goal, supported by the U.S. as the communist threat grew in Asia, was to get the economy back on its feet. The government established priorities for support and protection—basic industries such as electric power, coal, iron, and steel. But as the recovery progressed under this plan and Japan began to export more to the U.S., tensions built up into friction. Textiles were only the first issue. In 1969, Japan agreed to voluntary restraint of iron and steel exports to the U.S. By 1976, Japan accepted voluntary restraints on the export of color TV sets. At about that time, demands began to be heard in the U.S. that Japan should import more American products. In 1978, Japan agreed to raise import quotas of beef and oranges. Two years later, congresspersons were demanding that Japan limit its exports of automobiles. Restrictions on machine tools followed. Eventually semiconductors became the issue and Japan took the extraordinary step of promising to import a specific percentage of American products, even though Japanese businessmen complained that it should be left to them to decide what, and how much, to buy.

CHAPTER 4

A Change of Course

THERE IS NO SINGLE POINT AT WHICH it could be said that JETRO's mission changed. As we have seen, it had been chartered to promote exports. Year by year, exports had increased until the favorable balance of trade had become something of an embarrassment and an international problem. Had JETRO been too successful? It is not fair to deny credit where credit is due. But more likely the startling swing had been the result of natural change beyond the influence of any single government agency. Thus, perhaps it was inevitable that JETRO make a 180-degree change in course and focus on helping other nations to export to Japan.

In 1967, Japan's exports exceeded $10 billion. Three years later this figure had doubled, and in 1972 the nation's foreign currency reserves reached $16 billion. During 1971, Japan's trade surplus with the United States grew to $2.5 billion, 40 percent higher than the total trade imbalance of the three previous years.

Japanese business leaders were delighted by this trend. Newspaper editorials boasted that Japan's gross national product was the world's second largest and welcomed

In April 1954, JETRO opened its first overseas office on 5th Avenue in New York City near the Emfire State Building. There were a 300-square-meter exhibition hall on the first floor and office space on the second floor. Every day the Japanese flag, the Rising Sun, was hoisted with the Stars and Stripes, and together the two draped over 5th Avenue. In February 1974, JETRO moved its office to the 44th floor of the McGraw-Hill Building on the Avenue of the Americas. In this new office space, the exhibition hall was replaced by a large conference room.

reference to a new "economic giant." At the same time they complained about foreign demands that Japan liberalize its financial markets and remove import restrictions. The Japanese society that had been indoctrinated with the idea that exporting was the key to economic success still considered importing detrimental, a holdover from the days when it was critical to conserve foreign exchange. There was little recognition of the fact that trade must flow in both directions. Perhaps JETRO had been too successful in its export promotion program. The time had come to rethink its mission.

Strangely enough, it is not possible to identify the point at which JETRO's emphasis changed from promoting exports to encouraging imports. I don't recall that any special committee was set up, or that directors met, to decide—or even discuss—a change of course. It just happened over a period of time, and the change was gradual and natural so that it was accepted with almost no controversy.

JETRO can be likened to a ponderous ship whose momentum prevents it from changing course quickly in response to the captain's orders. In this case the JETRO ship did not have a captain with hands on the wheel. A course had been established in the beginning, and the crew, without further direction, saw to it that their vessel plowed ahead. But presently the winds and tides changed, shifting the ship's course a little at a time in a different direction, and no one became concerned.

The first JETRO offices overseas had been in expensive ground-floor locations where the Japanese flag was flown and all kinds of goods were on public display. They essentially were showcases for selling Japanese products.

As the first move overseas to emphasize imports, JETRO's Japan Trade Center in Bangkok changed its stance in 1969 and offices moved to less ostentatious quarters on an upper floor where conference rooms replaced exhibit space. A few years later the same was done in New York. The realization was growing within JETRO that buying was an effective way to develop sales in a friendly market—in other words that trade had to be reciprocal to be successful. Promotion of that concept required two public relations programs.

The first was to build a better image abroad of Japan, Japanese companies, and Japanese goods, particularly in the United States, which was Japan's primary trading partner. The purpose was to ensure that even with diminishing JETRO emphasis on sales, the market would continue to be healthy.

The second was to build a market for American goods in Japan and help Americans to find it. This second program was not in the minds of government leaders when they decided to organize JETRO, but experience made it only too clear that trade is a two-way street and Americans, for whatever reason, were having difficulty penetrating the Japanese market.

Gearing up for these changes, the Public Relations Division, which had been part of the Overseas Activities Department, was upgraded in October 1971 to an independent department with two divisions. I was appointed to head one of them. Two years later I was named director-elect of the entire PR Department. I thought the title was director-elect because at age forty-two I was considered too young to be a director. What I did not know was that I had been placed in the director class in anticipation of my next assignment, which required a person of some seniority. It took several years for the "elect" to be removed.

Up to this time, Japanese corporations doing business in America were only faceless giants with no visible presence other than the goods they marketed, like Toyota automobiles or Sony electronic products. Since then, Japanese companies have become associated with a variety of activities, including sponsorship of highly visible sports events. But at the time, the words "philanthropy" and "social responsibility" were virtually unknown in Japanese boardrooms, and the corporations were subjected to frequent criticism in the U.S. media for their lack of interest in the communities where they had found a home. Eager Japanese correspondents stationed in New York and Washington reported these comments in considerable detail. A number of books critical of Japan were published in the U.S. and were quickly translated and distributed in Japan.

Unfortunately, such criticism seemed to have little effect on the policy of Japanese corporations. I decided that if the whip didn't work, perhaps the carrot would. *Overseas Market* set out to report community activities of Japanese corporations in countries where they conducted business, of foreign companies in Japan, and of foreign corporations in their own countries. The idea was to recognize laudable programs and stimulate interest in launching similar projects. In an effort to include as many case studies as possible, we asked JETRO offices around the world to dig up information.

The result was not encouraging. There were numerous examples of American corporations contributing funds as well as the time of their employees in worthy projects in their own communities—projects like athletic leagues for youngsters, facilities for the elderly, support for libraries and school programs.

In Japan, corporate social responsibility dealt primarily with consumer protection, reducing industrial pollution, and cleaning up the environment. But we also learned that Mitsui Trading Co. was supporting a Little League program in Australia; that high school and college scholarships had been initiated by Mitsubishi, Mitsui, and Matsushita Electric in Southeast Asian nations; that a million-dollar donation had been made to Harvard University by the Mitsubishi group with Nissan Motor Co. making a similar gift; and that the Sumitomo Group had gone one better by giving $2 million to Yale. But these were primarily gifts of money, which, while gratefully received, lacked the human touch, as when American businesspeople took the time to coach youth teams or planted trees and flowers in public parks while their Japanese counterparts were enjoying themselves on the golf course.

The social responsibility issue of *Overseas Market* was not well received. Perhaps the subject was too far ahead of the times. One of its shortcomings was that it failed to point out strongly enough that money alone doesn't get the job done. As one American put it, "It is important to show your good will by giving money, but it is equally important to give of your time, skills and knowledge."

The Americans' gifts also showed considerable imagination. In 1963, Mobil Oil celebrated its seventieth year in Japan by sponsoring a writing contest for children based on the red horse, which, not so incidentally, was the company's trademark. The winning entries were published and the books distributed to the nation's schools. The Italian Olivetti company underwrote a documentary—which took eighteen months to complete—on the precious ancient city of Kyoto. Pepsi Cola not only sponsored a soccer program in Japanese schools but also started a training program for coaches. Not to be outdone, Coca-Cola started a campaign to beautify roadways by donating 30,000 metal trash baskets to towns and cities.

The second part of my department's mission—to help foreigners become aware of the Japanese market—also posed a major challenge. Up to that time, most of Japan's international communications were devoted to defending its trading practices in the face of foreign criticism, and were largely negative in tone. I felt the need for a simple, upbeat English-language brochure telling of the great opportunities to be found in exporting to Japan. I also knew that getting support for such a brochure would be difficult, mainly because there was no precedent for anything like it.

One day while I was mulling over ideas for the brochure, Jun Iida, the Japanese sales representative for the *New York Times*, came to see me. His mission was to sell advertising and he was a frequent visitor, although I made it clear each time that JETRO had no budget for buying space in a major publication like the *Times*.

"Iida-san," I said, "you are a persistent fellow, and you have given me an idea. If the *Times* could produce a brochure about business opportunities in Japan, I can guarantee that JETRO would purchase 10,000 copies."

Iida laughed and protested that the *Times* wasn't in the brochure business. Several weeks later he came to see me again. "The only reason I can see for JETRO not publishing its own brochure is that you don't have anyone to do it," he said. "Well, I have someone in mind who could do an excellent job."

A few days later Iida introduced me to Tate Ratcliff, who was a researcher for the Boston Consulting Group and a consultant to other American firms doing business in Japan. He had been in the country long enough to learn to read Japanese newspapers and even difficult government documents.

I told him what I had in mind and asked him to draft a text in English. Standard JETRO procedure at that time for producing English-language material was to have the text written in Japanese, then translated. Invariably this was a tedious, time-consuming process, with numerous experts examining and commenting on both versions and the result being a dull and perhaps confusing document. I didn't want to go through this kind of rigmarole. Besides, I figured that material directed to an English-speaking audience would be more effective if it were written originally in English rather than translated from another language. There was one other factor: I calculated that my superiors were more likely to approve the English draft without delay if there were no Japanese original for comparison.

Ratcliff gave me an estimate of the cost and in ten days produced a draft for a brochure to be titled "Japan as an Export Market." It was very close to what I had in mind, and I felt confident about distributing copies to various departments for the obligatory approval before proceeding with the printing.

But somehow, MITI got wind of the project and threw up a number of roadblocks. MITI officials demanded to see the Japanese original as well as the English draft. They expressed doubt that a foreigner could explain the Japanese market accurately, failing to understand that Japanese ineptitude was the reason I had sought outside help. They complained that there was no precedent for hiring a foreigner to draft a JETRO brochure. And they objected to the cost. At the time, the standard compensation for Japanese writers was ¥1,000 per page of copy. Japanese translators were paid ¥2,000 per page for converting the text into English, and a native English-speaker was paid ¥1,000 per page for correcting the translation. This totaled ¥4,000 per page. Ratcliff's normal charge for writing text in English was ten times that amount—¥40,000 per page. He agreed to ¥24,000—but still six times greater than what JETRO was accustomed to paying—because he believed in the project.

My belief in the importance of creating an interesting, attractive, lucid brochure overcame my uneasiness about the cost and I was determined to press on with the project. My desire to publish the brochure was based neither on market surveys or orders from above, but solely on my conviction that it was necessary. Somehow, someone higher up decided the brochure was a worthwhile project and approved it. Because no provision for it had been made in the 1971 budget, money had to be diverted from other projects. The first printing for Japan as an Export Market was 30,000 copies, which were quickly distributed to JETRO offices and Japanese embassies and consulates around the world, and to anyone who asked for them. Soon we had to order 20,000 more.

My friend Iida was so intrigued by the success of the project that he resigned from the *New York Times*, hired Ratcliff, and started his own company for producing brochures.

Iida's successor at the *Times* was a man named Kobayashi who came to me in December of 1971 with an interesting offer. He said he had been unable to sell all the

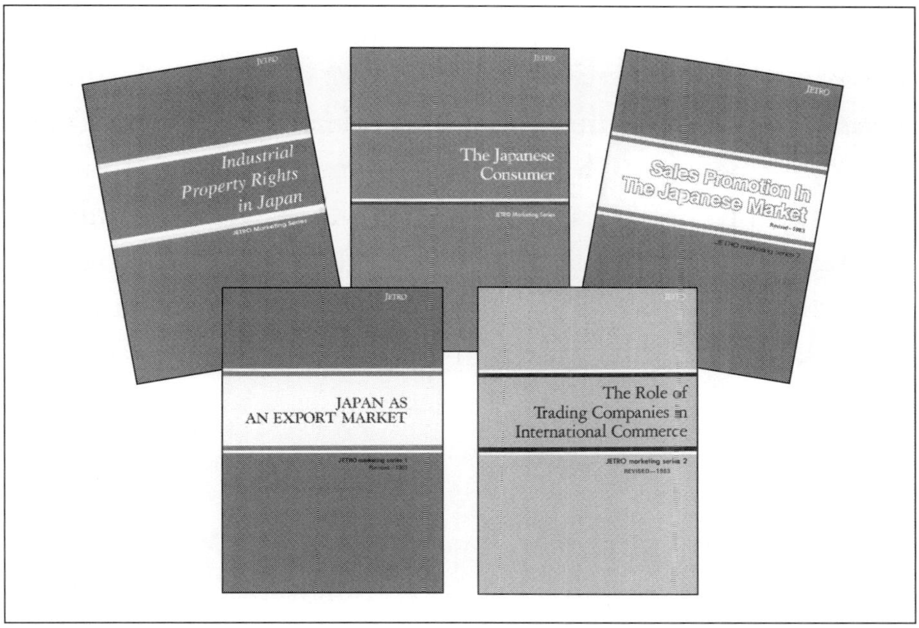

IN FEBRUARY 1971, THE FIRST ISSUE OF THE JETRO MARKETING SERIES, "JAPAN AS AN EXPORT MARKET," WAS COMPLETED. THE SERIES FOCUSED ON EXPLAINING THE JAPANESE MARKET TO FOREIGN BUSINESSMEN, AND THE ISSUE WAS THE SYMBOLIC FIRST PUBLICATION EXPRESSING A 180-DEGREE DIRECTIONAL CHANGE OF JETRO'S POLICY—FROM THE ORIGINAL EXPORT PROMOTION TO IMPORT PROMOTION—IN VISIBLE FORM. FEATURING EIGHTEEN DIFFERENT THEMES, THIS JETRO MARKETING SERIES WAS PUBLISHED UNTIL 1978. THE BOOKLETS WERE UPDATED AS THE NEED AROSE, AND EVEN TODAY THEY ARE STILL WIDELY USED AS USEFUL INFORMATION SOURCES.

advertising space in the newspaper's annual Asia-Pacific section and offered a small hole to JETRO without charge. It was of modest size, but large enough to invite readers to write in for a free copy of "Japan as an Export Market." We received more than 150 requests, some from as far away as Hong Kong and Brazil.

Although we did not seek publicity other than in the *New York Times*, we found stories about the brochure in such varied publications as *The Financial Times* of London, *Home Furnishings Daily* in the United States, *Edmonton Journal* in Canada, the *Investor* and *Bangkok Post* in Thailand, and *Financial Dagblad* in Holland. The American Embassy in Tokyo and the American Chamber of Commerce in Japan asked permission to reprint the brochure, which we were only too glad to do. In all, more than 100,000 copies of the booklet were distributed.

"Japan as an Export Market" became a public relation director's dream. It was the first of a series of eighteen booklets providing information that would help foreign businesspeople to enter the Japanese market with everything from agricultural and marine products, to apparel, to machinery, to environmental protection items. Iida-san, who had introduced JETRO to successful publishing, and his writer, Ratcliff, produced many of these booklets for us.

Then a strange thing happened. Suddenly I found I was being viewed as an expert in the new (to Japan) science of public relations. I began to receive requests for interviews, articles, and speeches. One day Kengo Otake of the *Nihon Keizai Shimbun* (Japan Economic Journal) told me his company would like to publish a guide for managing public relations overseas and asked me to write it. I was flattered. Not only did Japan need such a book, but it would add to JETRO's prestige.

But finding time for such a project was a problem. My typical workday was 9 A.M. to 10 or 11 P.M. Most offices were open a half day on Saturdays, but I was working until 5 or 6 P.M. In addition, JETRO was in charge of the Japanese government pavilion at the World's Fair to be held in Osaka. Although I was not directly involved, the fair would add to the burden of all JETRO employees. I asked Otake to give me time to think about the book.

This gave me an opportunity to review my qualifications for writing such a text. I had had no knowledge of public relations when I had been assigned to New York in 1962, but had learned something of my profession during my five years there. Then I had spent two years as director of the PR division in Tokyo. That was the extent of my experience. I had never formally studied public relations. Everything I had learned up to this point had been on the job.

There was no question that Japan and Japanese business in particular needed to learn that PR was more than sales promotion and advertising. How would I teach that lesson? There were perhaps a dozen books in Japanese available on public relations but most were translations of American books and failed to address Japan's special problems. If I accepted Otake's proposal, mine would the first book on overseas public relations by a Japanese for Japanese. With some misgivings I agreed to take the assignment.

Otake and I outlined five chapters. The first would demonstrate the difference between marketing and advertising on one hand, and public relations on the other. It would point out that a public relations program was not specifically a sales tool, but that such a program would create a better understanding of Japan and Japanese culture as a first step toward improving communications and, ultimately, sales.

Chapter 2 would emphasize the need for research. A public relations director had to know the customs, religious beliefs, language and cultural nuances of the target audience. He or she had to understand the goals of the plan, and be skilled in the art of communication.

Chapter 3 would report on successful public relations programs of major Japanese companies and analyze the reasons for their success.

Chapter 4 would target speech-making and developing printed materials and films.

Chapter 5 would provide tips on selecting a public relations firm, using the skills of an account executive, and dealing with the media. The advice would be basic. For example, my notes said of relations with newspapermen: "Cooperate with them, but avoid giving the impression you are trying to use them. Be precise with facts and figures. In press releases use short sentences."

Although these topics were elementary, they were new to the Japanese, and I agreed with Otake that the book would be useful. But I was quick to admit I wasn't qualified to write authoritatively on all the subjects.

That shortcoming could be solved by an idea that would also enhance JETRO's reputation. My thought was to invite other members of JETRO's PR staff to contribute material that I would integrate into the book. Then I could state in the preface that the book had been produced by the PR Division of JETRO's Overseas Activities Department, including members of overseas offices.

Otake objected. He said his company's books customarily were authored by individuals, and since I would be writing most of the text, I should appear as the sole author. I argued that whatever his company's policy might be, individual recognition should be considered inappropriate in books of broad scope such as this one. I pointed out that few newspaper articles carried the bylines of individual reporters and it was the custom for government reports to be credited only to a particular department.

Otake argued strongly that the practice only reinforced the international impression that Japan was a country of groups rather than individuals. I protested that if I were listed as sole author, I could be accused of using the assets of my organization for personal gain. Besides, I said, my objective was to enhance JETRO's reputation, and if I were given excessive credit, my position within the agency would become very difficult.

Finally, I showed Otake some books his company had published for organizations like the Industrial Bank of Japan and the Daiwa Bank Management Institute which were credited to the institutions rather than individual authors. Otake finally agreed to have my book credited to JETRO's Overseas Activities Department. Five months after the book's publication, the department's PR division was upgraded in JETRO's table of organization in obvious recognition of the work it was doing. I smiled as I wondered about the reaction of Michiro Uga, the MITI official who had been so negative about the value of PR activities at the budget hearings when I first took over my assignment. Otake said I was entitled to be compensated for my work, but I took payment in the form of copies of the book, which were distributed to JETRO's overseas offices, opinion leaders, and corporate public relations managers.

In 1994, more than two decades after the book was published, I received a letter from someone named Masakatsu Tomita. He enclosed a newspaper clipping that reported I had retired from JETRO and moved to Denver, Colorado, where I was planning to publish a monthly newsletter to be called *Understanding Japan*. He wrote that for more than fifteen years he had been an adviser to Japanese corporations operating in the United States. Then he asked, "Aren't you the Mr. Sogo who wrote the legendary book on overseas public relations published by Nikkei?"

The book had been out of print for years, but to hear that its message was still remembered was deeply gratifying.

CHAPTER 5

Japan on the *Today Show*

DURING THE YEARS I WAS IN NEW YORK, I was frustrated by the absence of "good" news about Japan in the American media. The news, if it wasn't about a natural disaster like an earthquake or a typhoon, seemed to be disagreeable such as the discovery of poisonous lead coloring in the feathers of Japanese-made Easter chicks. One of the few times we felt like cheering was when the press gave substantial space to consumer advocate Ralph Nader's report that Japanese automobiles were safe.

The leading daytime television program at the time was NBC's *Today Show*, which was telecast from 7 to 9 A.M. every weekday. It was an interesting combination of news and features with Barbara Walters and Hugh Downs as hosts. Several times we tried to get their producers interested in doing a feature on Japan, but without success.

About a year after I was reassigned to Tokyo, we received a call from the New York office saying they had an inquiry from NBC about the possibility of doing some *Today Show* programs from Japan. I was elated and pledged to do everything possible to bring Walters and Downs and associates to Japan. It was to take three long years for the arrangements to be completed.

During this time I wondered often what had changed NBC's mind about featuring Japan. Several events had taken place to bring American attention to Japan. In 1964, Tokyo had hosted the Olympic Games while at the same time introducing the swift and innovative Shinkansen bullet trains racing between Tokyo and Osaka. In 1967, Japan achieved its target of $10 billion in exports, and just three years later became the third nation, behind the United States and West Germany, with more than $20 billion in exports. Also in 1970, Japan's second largest city, Osaka, hosted EXPO 70, which firmly established the country as an industrially advanced nation. For years preceding this period much of the world had recognized Japan only as the nation totally defeated in World War II. NBC obviously wanted to portray the contemporary "real" Japan. Whatever the reason, we at JETRO were delighted and excited at the prospect of the *Today Show* featuring Japan for a vast American audience.

Two major problems, which shouldn't have been difficult at all, had to be solved before JETRO could formally invite NBC to Japan.

The first was an agreement from NHK (Nippon Hoso Kyokai), the government-subsidized Japanese national network, to cooperate with NBC. My colleagues and I visited NHK's offices many times to negotiate during the six months that preceded the agreement. The reasons given for delaying approval were always vague. It was not until years later that

I learned what had held up the pact. First, there had been many debates within NHK's hierarchy over whether it was legal for a semiofficial entity to work with a private foreign company. Eventually the matter was taken before Yoshinori Maeda, chairman of NHK's board, for the final decision and he lost no time in giving approval. Today NHK routinely cooperates with many foreign networks in coproducing and exchanging programs.

The second problem was money. NBC expected extensive, costly cooperation and JETRO's total budget for helping foreign media organizations to make films about Japan was an unbelievably paltry $3,000. Under the Japanese system each government agency's budget was very strictly controlled, as demonstrated in my encounter with Mr. Uga of MITI, and funds were not transferable from one project to another except in very rare cases. Fearing the worst, I took my problem to Zenzo Tobinaga, the MITI official with oversight over JETRO. Fortunately he understood the public relations value of the NBC visit and my problem. Slashing fearlessly through red tape, he squeezed small amounts out of various budget items. Within an hour he had earmarked $120,000 for the NBC project—40 times more than I had started with. He showed an understanding and flexibility virtually unknown at the time in the Japanese bureaucracy.

An unexpected international development helped a little. When President Nixon took the U.S. off the gold standard as part of what Japan called the "Nixon Shocks," major countries had to allow their currencies to "float." This means the exchange rate is not controlled. The yen-dollar exchange rate changed from ¥360 to $1 to ¥308 to $1, which meant the yen currency at my disposal would go further.

NBC's advance party came to Japan for two weeks in August 1971 to lay the groundwork. The main party of thirty-four, all of them requiring help, arrived September 28 and stayed until October 7. In Tokyo they were housed in the luxurious Takanawa Prince Hotel. JETRO assigned seven of the PR staff to the NBC party and hired fifteen interpreters, mostly young men and women who had studied in the States. In addition, NHK provided thirty-five persons, mainly technicians.

Today, television programs can be transmitted instantaneously and live to viewers from anywhere in the world. In 1971, exposed film was flown to New York, where it was developed and edited before being broadcast. The Japan series was telecast daily in the United States from October 4 to October 8 over 220 stations, an audience of staggering proportions.

NBC had total editorial control of the product, but depended on us to arrange interviews, suggest locations for photography, negotiate permission for using the sites, and all the logistics such as transportation, housing, and meals. The program was to be divided into three parts: Japan's "past" to be taped in Kyoto, the ancient capital; its "present" in bustling Tokyo; and its "future" in the rebuilt Hiroshima and Kusatsu, a developing area on the shores of Lake Biwa.

In the "past" segment, Hugh Downs at magnificent Heian Shrine explained the history and architecture of the shrine itself, talked about Shinto and Japanese mythology, and described with proper visuals the symbolism in traditional wedding ceremonies. With displays of arts and crafts he briefly reviewed Japanese history from the Heian period (A.D. 794-1185) to the beginning of the modern era with the Meiji Restoration (1868).

The program also discussed the role and lifestyle of the imperial family and court music and dance. At Kyoto's Tenryuji Temple, two American Buddhist priests discussed differences among Buddhism, Zen and Christianity as practiced in the States. In the temple gardens, Barbara Walters, looking quite at ease in an elaborate kimono, discussed the traditional costume and contrasted it with Western-style fashions by Hanae Mori, Japan's best-known designer. The camera took viewers inside a traditional Japanese home with

IN 1971, JOE GARAGIOLA, BARBARA WALTERS AND HUGH DOWNS FILMED A FEW EPISODES OF THE *TODAY SHOW* IN JAPAN. THE VENTURE TOOK GREAT EFFORT TO COORDINATE BUT EXPOSED A CONTEMPORARY AND REAL JAPAN TO A VAST AUDIENCE IN AMERICA.

commentators explaining the various features and a look at handicrafts such as silk textiles, dolls, ivory carvings, porcelain, and calligraphy. Inside the temple an English-language professor from Doshisha University, Harold Hamada, explained the significance of kendo, fencing with long bamboo swords. And finally a geisha named Miyosaku talked about her life as an entertainer and the importance of geisha as custodians of traditional performing arts.

The past and present were brought together by Joe Garagiola, the former big league baseball player who was a member of the *Today* team, when he interviewed Jesse Takamiyama, a Hawaiian who had moved to Japan and become a sumo wrestling champion. Takamiyama related the history of sumo and the lifestyle in the organization or "stable" of which he was a member, and the traditions that still govern the sport. Garagiola also interviewed Clifton Curfew, an American woodblock printer, and his wife, Louise, about living in Japan and adjusting to Japanese ways.

One segment of the second installment, on modern Japan, was taped in the roof garden of the Daimaru department store with a panorama of the Tokyo skyline in the background. Dr. Chie Nakane, professor of social anthropology at Tokyo University, talked about changing manners in modern Japan, male-female relationships, labor and management problems, and the outlook of college students. Robert Strickland, an American married to a Japanese and owner of a Tokyo restaurant, was interviewed about his life in Japan, arranged marriages, and the problems of rearing a child of mixed blood in a homogeneous society. And Yoshiya

Ariyoshi, president of a large shipping company, discussed the employment system and the Japanese way of doing business. By contrast, in a startling demonstration of the Americanization of Japanese culture, a rock group called The Peanuts performed one of their hit songs.

Of course politics and pontificating were part of the *Today Show* melange. Four Tokyo journalists were asked to discuss politics, economics, and the sometimes rocky relations between the United States and Japan. They were Richard Halloran of the *New York Times*; William Hartley of the *Wall Street Journal*; Masaru Ogawa, the American-born editor of the *Japan Times*; and John Rich, who covered the Far East for NBC News. All four were articulate and knowledgeable, and contributed much to an understanding of problems facing the United States and Japan.

John Rich also interviewed Prime Minister Eisaku Sato in his official residence. During the three months leading up to NBC's visit, there had been two major incidents that from the Japanese viewpoint had a strong negative impact on relations with the U.S. One was President Nixon's abruptly announced new economic policy, which hurt Japanese exports. The other was the delay in sharing with Japan information about Nixon's intent to visit communist China, with which the U.S. long had been at odds. This delay was interpreted in Tokyo as a sign of American distrust of its most important partner in East Asia.

John Rich asked the prime minister whether he thought President Nixon should stop in Japan on his way to China.

Sato was expressionless as he replied, "It won't be necessary."

Rich then asked whether Sato thought Nixon should stop in Japan on his trip back to the U.S.

"It won't be necessary," Sato repeated coldly. "He can do whatever he wants."

Nixon's slight was seen in Japan as a calculated sign of American displeasure over continued U.S.-Japanese trade friction.

The third segment was filmed at Peace Park in Hiroshima, where the war-ending nuclear attack is commemorated. This could have been a delicate matter and I was worried, but it turned out very well. Mayor Setsuo Yamada of Hiroshima discussed popular Japanese opposition to rearmament. A famous antibomb poem by Sankichi Toge was read. It begins "Bring back my father…" Three survivors of the nuclear attack were interviewed along with a young officer from Japan's Self Defense Force.

The only serious glitch was in Tokyo. It developed over one simple issue, and at the time I was convinced it took years from my life.

NBC's producers had selected the Nissan automobile company's spectacular showroom on the Ginza at one of Japan's busiest corners to tape interviews on a Sunday afternoon for an important part of the "present" segment. The entire Ginza street is closed to vehicular traffic on Sundays and the area is jammed with pedestrian shoppers. NBC wanted to conduct several interviews in the showroom with crowds of Japanese walking by in the background. This would require that the huge plate-glass windows be removed so the Nissan cars on display could be moved out. Nissan officials were promised all this would be done at NBC's expense with the least possible disruption. They had agreed reluctantly and it appeared all was in readiness, until one Nissan executive asked in passing who would be interviewed. Well, said the NBC producer, there would be Kumiko Torikai, a well-known Japanese TV personality, several militant left-wing and right-wing college students, and several others, including Tokyo's governor Ryokichi Minobe. Minobe was a leader of the Socialist Party, the first socialist to be elected governor of Tokyo, and a widely known advocate of drastic measures to combat air pollution.

Minobe's name brought up the Nissan officials with a start. One of them, clearing his throat, said quite firmly, "We cannot permit you to use the Nissan showroom if Governor Minobe is to be interviewed."

Environmental pollution had become a major issue in Japan a year before the NBC visit. In 1970 one in four Japanese households owned an automobile, and traffic fatalities and injuries had set records. Photochemical smog cast a pall over Tokyo. Toxic sludge had been discovered being dumped into the sea, cyanide was found in the Tama River flowing through Tokyo, and it was charged that the rice being sold was contaminated with traces of cadmium and chemical insecticides. Hurriedly the national government had established an environmental protection agency. Nissan was understandably nervous about the possibility of the outspoken Governor Minobe attacking the automobile industry from their showroom.

When I suggested another site, the NBC producer, Stewart Shulberg, said it was too late to make a change. The clock was ticking and I had to find a solution quickly.

Nissan understood the problem and agreed to withdraw their objection if NBC could guarantee there would be no discussion about air pollution with Governor Minobe.

NBC balked. The *Today Show* was a news program, I was reminded, and NBC had no control over what might be said during an interview. NBC could neither promise not to ask about pollution nor guarantee that Governor Minobe would not talk about it.

I explained this to the Nissan people but they were not satisfied. Eventually Nissan agreed that NBC's conditions were acceptable if not entirely satisfactory. But the issue was so sensitive that the Nissan representatives asked JETRO—not NBC—to sign a statement to the effect that Governor Minobe would not be asked about automobile air pollution. On the strength of a hint by an NBC writer that he would not include the question in the script for the interviewer, I drafted a statement that was duly signed by JETRO's executive director, and his seal affixed to make it official. The interviewers did not bring up the subject of air pollution and Governor Minobe found other matters to talk about. I almost collapsed in relief when the taping session ended.

To conclude the series, NBC's three commentators summarized their impressions of Japan. Downs said that of the more than a dozen countries *Today* had featured during his tenure, Japan was the most impressive. He said he saw virtually no relationship between the traditional arts and culture and the nation's highly advanced industrial technology. Barbara Walters said she had come to Japan expecting it to be quaintly Oriental, but had found it impressively modern, citing the Bullet Train, which ran at an average speed of 120 miles an hour, spotless hotels, and superb service. She added that she had no doubt that the 21st century would be the era of Japan and the Japanese people. Garagiola remarked that he was most impressed by Hiroshima. Having walked through Arlington National Cemetery just outside Washington, D.C., where American service veterans are buried, and then having visited Hiroshima, Garagiola said he had to ask himself why it had been necessary for the two countries to fight a war.

My colleagues in Japan and I were pleased that NBC's visit had gone so well, but we were ecstatic to learn how well the series had been received in the United States. A Nielsen survey showed that more than 3.3 million households had seen the series, an audience three times that of the closest competing program. We had reached a large segment of America with an entertaining, accurate, and informative story of contemporary Japan. All the hard work and worry in preparation for the project had been worthwhile. The door had been opened for other segments of the American media to take an interest in Japan.

Working so closely with a high-powered and high-level American organization also had benefited my associates and me. We learned much about the American way of thinking, behavior patterns, and power dynamics. We Japanese were accustomed to the slow "from the bottom up" system of decision-making, in which a group of mid-level managers comes up with an idea, drafts a plan, and takes it to top management for formal approval. It was eye-opening to see how much authority the American executive producer on the scene had over his staff. I wondered, without ever arriving at a conclusion, whether the Japanese system was democratic since everyone was involved in the decision-making process, and whether the American system was autocratic. But it would also seem that if Americans could make decisions at the working level, this was democracy in action.

What was most important, though, was that working together on a very important project, Americans and Japanese had shared both joy and hardship and learned to trust each other.

Chapter 6

Women to the Rescue

Although JETRO was well in advance of most other Japanese organizations in using the skills of people who were not Japanese, it took a major problem to break down the unofficial but rigid barrier against hiring a foreign woman.

The problem was correspondence. JETRO's Tokyo office received a large volume of mail from abroad, most of it in English. And most of the letters required response without delay. But our system was so cumbersome and slow that our replies to inquiries often were sent out too late to be useful. Sometimes we were accused of not answering our mail at all.

The cause was a policy that required a person to respond to a letter in Japanese if he or she were not comfortable in English. Then it would be translated by someone else, and finally it would be sent to a so-called English expert for double-checking. Even I had to draft my letters in English in longhand, then submit them to an expert for review. The corrected letters were then circulated for approval by all managers with any involvement in the matters touched upon.

After everyone had passed on it, the letter was retyped and returned to the original author for signature prior to mailing.

If our overseas correspondents had been aware of what was involved even in a simple reply to an inquiry, they might have been more understanding of our tardiness in responding. As it was, much correspondence probably went unanswered because it didn't make sense to go through the entire elaborate process to send routine acknowledgments or thank-you notes.

JETRO's inefficiency bothered me. During my time in New York, I had become impressed by the way Americans communicated through letters and written memos that provided a record for future reference. After discussing even minor matters with American businessmen, I would usually receive a letter in a day or two confirming the contents of our conversation. I learned that even in their personal lives Americans sent cards and notes for birthdays, anniversaries, and other happy occasions, or simply to say hello. Of course these Americans were corresponding in their native language; it was simple for us to respond to inquiries in Japanese, which we did routinely. But we were in the business of dealing with non-Japanese and struggling with the intricacies of what to us was a very difficult foreign language and a daunting, exhausting, and time-consuming process. No doubt many Japanese businesses faced the same problem.

I felt the matter of responding to letters was important enough that two articles on the subject were published in *Overseas Market*. In one of them an American PR consultant presented examples of ways to respond to requests for information, brochures, or for details that were not easily available.

These articles did not help us very much in JETRO and I doubt that they were of great use to others.

I believed the solution to our internal problem was simple: hire a competent foreigner with secretarial training and let this person take the responsibility for shortcutting work that was taking so much of our time. But if the solution was simple, it was not easy. Few foreigners, least of all women, were employed in Japan's government or business offices. I decided it was time for change. I went directly to MITI, explained my problem, and asked for authority to hire a foreign woman as a part-time secretary.

As expected, the answer was a flat no. Such a thing had never been done, I was told, and it would be an unnecessary luxury in view of the number of current employees proficient in English. That was news to me. I argued that I wasn't trying to pad my staff or make my job easier, but rather wanted to improve JETRO's efficiency and enhance its image. Such a secretary, I said, would help the offices of the chairman, the executive director, and department directors. Still the answer was no.

One day several months later, the Planning Department informed me that MITI had sent instructions that JETRO was to hire a foreigner as secretary for my department.

"Impossible," I said. "I requested a secretary not long ago and was turned down flat."

"Yes," I was told, "we know that. But whatever has happened has happened, and these instructions have now come from MITI."

Of course I didn't argue the matter further. Later I learned that MITI's executive director had written a letter

昭和47年（1972年）1月7日　金曜日

日米関係

「東京・渋谷のデパート裏の、三畳で万年床に住んでます」

朝食　七十円のみそ汁に、ご飯。

昼食　チョコレート。

夕食　ニッポン風ケーキ。

もっぱら、外食している。

メリンダ・ユーイング嬢は、六日、日本貿易振興会（ジェトロ）海外PR部に初出勤した。

「おれの新案特許、買うのはいないか」（ベルギー）

「工場、たたき売りたし」（米国）

経済大国ニッポンに情報を求める商会状への返事書きが、新人秘書メリンダ嬢のおもな仕事である。

「アルバイトです」という。午前中と夜間、英会話学校で先生をしている。午後、ジェトロの机にすわる。

郷里の米オハイオ州ヤングスター市から、二カ月前、来日した。「鉄鋼の会社の町です。でも、ニッポンの鉄鋼に負けそうです」。ハーバードでロシア文学を専攻したが、日本語もうまい。こんなしゃれをいう。

「私、ヤングスターのコーガイ（郊外）に住んでますが、市内はコーガイ（公害）、同じですね」

昭和二十三年生れ。「母によると、米国人は米国に住み、米国人と結婚すべきだそうです。私、三十歳まで外国にいたい。若いうちは、その方がいいですよね」

日米関係について。

「ニッポンはアメリカになるんじゃないですか。日本の友人のおかあさん、深いおじぎ、お茶の作法、すばらしい。私の友人、おじぎも、お茶も、だめで、私みたい。世界中がアメリカみたいになっちゃ、ほんと面白くないわ」

彼女の机に、まだタイプライターはない。秘書はみつかったが、お役所仕事で納入が間に合わないんだそうだ。

As soon as JETRO Tokyo office hired Melinda Ewing, a Japanese newspaper reporter came to interview her. The next day, a long article with her photo was featured in the mass circulation newspaper *The Asahi Shimbun*. Today, a foreigner working in a Japanese office is not unusual, but it was news in 1972. Courtesy of *The Asahi Shimbun*.

in English and had someone on his staff bring it to JETRO to have it checked by a native English-speaker. When told that JETRO had no such employee, he declared it was ridiculous that a government agency heavily involved in foreign trade should not have at least one native English-speaker.

Before long I hired a young woman named Melinda Ewing who had been recommended by a public relations consulting firm. She was to have a profound influence on JETRO.

Melinda had a degree in Russian literature from Harvard but was teaching English mornings and evenings in Tokyo. She agreed to work for us every afternoon. She spoke a reasonable amount of Japanese and was anxious to learn more. Her employment by JETRO was unusual enough that Hiroshi Aoki, an *Asahi* newspaper reporter, wrote a story that was published together with a photograph of Melinda. Aoki's story noted that JETRO had hired a secretary, but because of bureaucratic red tape she had not been provided with a typewriter. A typewriter appeared the very next day.

Melinda introduced JETRO to an entirely new culture. She surprised us by coming to work wearing sandals and carrying a backpack. She had her lunch in a paper bag and usually ate at her desk. She was so completely natural about her informality that she was quickly accepted. Her knowledge of Japanese enabled her to fit in comfortably in the office routine, and of course her ability to correct and type our awkwardly written English letters quickly was nothing short of wonderful. When the work piled up, she willingly stayed late, sharing a quick meal of noodles with the rest of the staff. She was simply one of us on occasions when the staff went on a weekend outing to a hot springs resort. We were despondent when Melinda decided it was time to move on. She had been a pioneer in breaking a foolish ethnocentric barrier. Today it is common to see foreigners working in public and private Japanese offices. In fact, under a government program to bring native English-speakers to Japan for a year as assistant English-language teachers in middle and high schools, the best qualified are offered positions as advisers in state government offices.

Despite the problem we had in hiring Melinda Ewing, JETRO has been considered among the leaders in giving women employment opportunities. Even so, until fiscal year 1999 there was a quota for the number of men and the number of women to be taken on. Each fall, hopeful young men and women in their very best clothes would visit JETRO to submit job applications, and the lucky ones would report for work at the beginning of the new fiscal year on April 1.

JETRO was more democratic about employment than most government agencies and firms. Many large corporations made no secret of their preference for graduates from certain elite universities. Others were known to open their doors more easily to relatives or friends of top executives. There was a term for this practice: *enko,* meaning "family connection." For some reason—perhaps the fact that JETRO was a fairly new government agency not burdened by tradition—these practices were not recognized.

Despite JETRO's relatively enlightened policies, women employees were not given the same opportunities as men. Generally, they were regarded as temporary hires who would resign in a few years after marriage, and usually were given only unimportant clerical work with little opportunity for promotion.

It was not unusual for someone who telephoned the Overseas PR Department to ask discreetly if not openly to speak to a male—any male—if a woman answered. Having seen how efficiently and competently American women performed in business, I was eager to give women in Japan the opportunity to take on important responsibilities, but it was not easy, for reasons ingrained in the Japanese culture. However, times change. The cabinet of Prime Minister Junichiro Koizumi seated in April 2001, included five women with one, Makiko Tanaka, in the important role of foreign minister.

Each summer since 1975, the Japan Business Association of Southern California had sent ten American teachers to Japan for two weeks to acquaint them with the country. JETRO had cooperated with the project from the beginning. A member of the staff would be given the assignment of coordinating the project, scheduling meetings, drawing up an itinerary, making hotel and meal arrangements, traveling with the group, and serving as a "mother hen." This assignment was a great opportunity not only to assume responsibility for an important project but also to get to know and understand Americans. In 1980 I assigned a newly hired woman whom I will call Kiyomi to take on this project. She had studied American and English literature in college, had a pleasant personality, and I was confident she would do a good job as well as benefit greatly from the experience. She was delighted.

The next day, I received a call from Kiyomi's mother. After the usual apologies, she told me she did not want her daughter to take on the assignment of escorting the American visitors. It was too great a responsibility for a young girl who had never traveled by herself.. And she said she considered it improper for an unmarried woman from a good family to be traveling with a group of foreigners which might include men.

My assurance that the assignment was quite proper, and a fine opportunity for her daughter, made no impression. The next day Kiyomi asked to be relieved of the assignment because of her mother's opposition. I had no choice but to take her off the project.

Overcoming gender-based barriers proved to be a difficult project because of long-standing customs observed almost unconsciously by the men and women themselves. For example, at the time I retired from JETRO in 1990, the men sat on one side of the auditorium and the women automatically went to the other side when new employees assembled for the ceremony observing their entry into the organization. Now, new employees sit in alphabetical order.

The separation of the sexes continues even after retirement from JETRO. Male retirees have an association called OB-Kai (Old Boy Society), which meets for a reunion each July 24. Women retirees become members of OG-Kai (Old Girl Society), which meets on the last Friday of October. Never do they meet together.

But slowly, opportunities for women are improving. In 1987, Sumiko Oike became the first woman in JETRO to reach managerial status when she was promoted from assistant director of the Secretarial Sservice Division to senior researcher. That move was considered important enough to be included in the top ten news events of the year listed in the JETRO newsletter. In 1988, the thirtieth anniversary of JETRO's founding, Hiromi Kusano was sent to England as JETRO's first female overseas trainee. The same year, Terue Tokoro went to Singapore as the first woman assigned to an overseas office. As of November 2000, there were six women working in overseas JETRO offices (Chicago, Toronto, Melbourne, Manila, and two in Singapore), and in the Tokyo head office there are seven women division directors, two directors, and eleven project managers. In local offices in Japan, women are chief directors in Aomori and Okayama.

Let me emphasize that I do not believe any person has to achieve managerial status to be successful. I am talking about opportunity to be of service, and in this regard women with ingenuity and kindness and dedication can be extremely successful even though they do not sit in a managerial chair.

Take my friends Mayumi Suzuki and Akiyo Yokoi, for example. In 1971 a small public relations firm called Press International, which often provided services for JETRO, suggested that an office be set up in central Tokyo to help foreign visitors on business missions. They put together a cooperative venture under which the Imperial Hotel provided space for a service center, Japan Air Lines paid overhead costs, and JETRO was responsible for a staff to provide information and help businesspeople make appointments, follow up business leads, and find their way around the city. JETRO had no one qualified to staff what was called JAL's Executive Service Lounge, so Press International recruited

Mayumi and Akiyo for us. The project was a huge success, largely because of the know-how, efficiency, and diligence of the two women, who somehow were able to solve even the most difficult problems of foreign businesspeople, many of whom were totally at a loss in an unfamiliar country with unfamiliar customs.

These young women were so good at their work, so pleasant and helpful, that they made themselves indispensable in Tokyo and later in Los Angeles.

As much as I have worked for equal opportunity for men and women, I discovered that old habits die hard. In 1980 I was invited to speak at the Kansai (Osaka) chapter of the American Chamber of Commerce on the subject of getting along smoothly with Japanese staff. In the question-and-answer period an American woman asked, "What is the best way for American managers to establish better communication with the Japanese staff?"

"Well," I replied, "in JETRO we try to maintain good communication through the concept of *ringi,* in which the draft of any idea or policy is passed around to all parties concerned for study, comment, and approval. In addition, we have frequent meetings. All section chiefs meet every Friday to discuss their activities and learn about what each of them is doing. Directors meet every Tuesday, and all executives meet every Thursday."

And then I added: "In my department, everyone meets on Monday. Even the women are invited."

The room burst into laughter, and I knew I had been guilty of an embarrassing faux pas.

Chapter 7

Los Angeles Assignment

In the summer of 1974 I was notified that I would be going back to the United States as director general of the Los Angeles office, one of JETRO's major overseas posts. My task as head of a large branch on only my second assignment outside Japan was a great challenge. During the eight years I had been working in Tokyo, Japan's trade situation—and JETRO's mission—had changed drastically. My new responsibilities were less to promote Japanese exports than to make friends among Americans and help them to sell in Japan.

But on my very first day, I discovered the JETRO office was confused and badly in need of leadership. There were twelve Japanese in the office but only three were JETRO personnel. Six were employees of prefectural governments who had been assigned to JETRO for the experience of working abroad. Three were on loan to JETRO from the Ministries of Finance; International Trade and Industry; and Agriculture, Fisheries and Forestry. Each of them seemed to be going his separate way without understanding the need for specific assignments. On my first morning at the office I called a staff meeting to introduce myself and ask for comments that would help us work more efficiently. In such a situation Japanese normally are reluctant to talk, so I was pleased when one of the local government representatives raised his hand. But he surprised me when he began to speak.

"I have never been happy with the way our responsibilities in this office are assigned," he said. "JETRO personnel get interesting jobs like research and public relations, while those of us from prefectural governments get meaningless work such as providing business information or helping American firms that don't seem to know anything about trade or Japanese markets. This is not fair. We should be treated as the equals of JETRO personnel. I request the new director general to review this policy."

His comment could be seen as arrogance, but I appreciated his frankness. It was evident that at least some of the non-JETRO personnel did not understand JETRO's mission and felt they were discriminated against. I had a job to do.

"Since I have just arrived," I said as calmly as I could, "I am unfamiliar with your various responsibilities. I will look into your complaint. Meanwhile, I want you to understand that JETRO considers providing business information and supporting American businesses seeking Japanese markets a very important function. If you feel that these duties are boring and demeaning, you probably are not the right person for this office."

A few days later I received further confirmation that something was amiss, and it came from Jack Whitehouse, a man I liked as a person and respected for his judgment.

Whitehouse was JETRO's PR consultant in Los Angeles. I had come to know him well during my days in the Overseas Public Relations Department in Tokyo, and we could be frank with each other. Over lunch, he urged me to give high priority to a shake-up of my information section.

"I often hear complaints from American businesspeople that JETRO doesn't return calls," he said, "and the information JETRO sends them isn't all that useful. I don't have to tell you how damaging that is."

I found that the six local government representatives, even though their English-language skills were quite inadequate, had been put in charge of the information section. They ran it with the help of young, inexperienced Americans hired as clerks. The young people were untrained and could not be expected to have any useful knowledge of international business. None had ever been to Japan. No wonder some of the staff thought the information section was unimportant.

The situation required early action, but what could I do with my very tight budget? Then I remembered Mayumi Suzuki and Akiyo Yokoi, the two young women from the Press International PR firm, whose diligence and enthusiasm had made the Executive Service Lounge at the Imperial Hotel such a success. They had the know-how about Japanese business, and the personality that my office needed. But without funds, how could I bring them to Los Angeles?

Out of near desperation I wrote to Rihachiro Shioyama, president of Press International who, as a result of the Service Lounge success, was highly regarded by JETRO as a public relations consultant. I told him my problem and asked whether there was any way the two women could be assigned to Los Angeles for a year or two.

He replied about a month later. In essence, he said that he was appreciative of his relationship with JETRO, that he was enthusiastic about the possibility of developing a wider clientele for his firm, that he had decided to open a Press International office in Los Angeles, and that if I would hire his company as our public relations counsel, he would assign Mayumi and Akiyo to work in our information office.

It was a great idea except for one problem: I already had a very competent PR consultant in Jack Whitehouse and was in no position to hire a second one. I had to make a decision and it was one of the most difficult I have ever made. After wrestling with the problem for several days, I invited Jack to lunch. I reminded him of the advice he had given me about JETRO's information section and told him about the possibility of getting two very competent women from Japan who would be the solution to my problems.

"Wonderful," he exclaimed. Then he saw the look on my face and asked, "What's the matter?"

"Well," I said, "in a way it's all your fault." I was trying to joke, but it didn't work. I told him that to get the women I would have to hire Press International, and because of my budget restrictions that meant I could not renew my contract with Whitehouse Associates.

Jack was quiet for a moment, then said: "You're making the right decision. I've tried for many years to get JETRO to do something about the information service, and you are the first to take action. If my advice is good, and I think it is, you have no choice but to hire the firm that will serve you best. And don't worry about me. Whitehouse Associates has plenty of other business to keep me busy.

"I have just one request," he went on. "I would like to see you occasionally even after our contract ends."

About a month later, Press International opened a Los Angeles branch and Mayumi and Akiyo came to our office. The improvement was almost instantaneous and I began to receive compliments instead of complaints. Jack Whitehouse dropped in one day about six months after the reorganization and told me with some pride that he had received many compliments about the improvement in JETRO's service. Some years later, Mayumi became deputy executive director of the Japan Business Association of Southern California, married, and then started her own firm, MS Research, in Los Angeles. Akiyo also married and became chief buyer for a San Francisco department store.

CHAPTER 8

Nick the Lion

ONE OF THE GOALS I HAD SET FOR MYSELF in Los Angeles was something that I had been unable to do in New York—to take part in community activities outside of business. That opportunity came during my first week on the job in the form of a telephone call from a man who identified himself as Gene Choy, president-elect of the Los Angeles Lions Club.

Choy explained that the Lions were a worldwide service organization with a membership of men dedicated to improving the communities in which they lived and worked. He said several of my predecessors at JETRO had been members and he wanted to meet me for lunch and explain Lions activities in greater detail so that I could consider joining.

I had hoped to join a service club but didn't know enough about them to have a preference. Since the Lions were the first to approach me, I was pleased to accept Choy's invitation.

He turned out to be a friendly, personable Chinese American. He explained the Lions' program of community service and philanthropy that underlies the fun and fellowship of weekly meetings. He said his club had about 200 members at one time, but the number had dwindled to about half that as young men joining the club were not numerous enough to replace those dropping out.

The following Friday, I presented myself at the Biltmore Hotel for the Lions' weekly lunch meeting. They were a boisterous bunch. A greeter at the room's entrance called out each member's name as he approached, and another fellow picked out a large identification button from a box. Someone was playing lively piano music. Several men introduced themselves, shook my hand, asked my name, and welcomed me. Nothing like this would happen in Japan.

Gene Choy found me, pulled me into a corner, and in a loud whisper asked, "Quick, Mr. Sogo, what is your nickname?"

LUNCHEON MEETING OF THE LIONS CLUB–LOS ANGELES CHAPTER. WHEN WE HAD VISITORS FROM JAPAN, I OFTEN TOOK THEM TO A LIONS CLUB MEETING.

"I don't have one," I replied. "Everyone calls me Mr. Sogo, or Sogo-san."

"That won't do." He thought a moment and then said, "Your name is going to be Nick."

So I became Nick Sogo. Later Gene Choi explained he couldn't think of a good name for me and had just shortened "nickname" to "Nick." I became known as Nick to all my non-Japanese friends in Los Angeles, and even today when I receive a card or letter beginning "Dear Nick," I know immediately where it is from.

The meeting was opened with the Pledge of Allegiance to the American flag, which was displayed at the front of the room. I am not a U. S. citizen and had no business pledging allegiance to the flag of a country other than mine, but this was a situation I had encountered many times while visiting schools in New York. I stood at attention with all the others in respect for the American flag but did not salute.

Before the meal was served I was introduced as a new Lion, to be known as Nick Sogo, and was given a loud and friendly welcome. They had adopted me immediately as one of them, which again is something that would not happen in Japan.

At first the noisy camaraderie surprised me, particularly the ritual of fining members as a way of replenishing the treasury. At the end of the meal a member called the "tail-twister" would rise and rattle a shiny tin bucket. Somebody would yell something like "Last Tuesday I saw Larry at a newsstand looking at a nudist magazine." "Fine him, fine him," the others would shout, and Larry, grinning widely, would drop a dollar in the bucket. Another member might shout, "Gene got two birdies last week." That would bring out calls of "Fine, fine," and Gene would pay up.

The only serious time was when the day's guest speaker took a half hour or so to bring us a message. The quiet periods gave me an opportunity to look around and I soon discovered I was the only Japanese member. I felt a little as though I were an ambassador from both JETRO and Japan. But I soon realized I was the only person who saw me as different; for the others I was just another fellow Lion.

I spent as much time as I could spare, and perhaps a bit more, in Lions activities. I seldom missed a meeting. On "White Cane Day," I volunteered for duty at the Eye Mobile, where the public came for free glaucoma tests. One of the members, Bruce Guthrie, told me, "Nick, if all Japanese people participated in community activities like you do, Japan would have fewer problems in the United States." That made me feel my time was being well spent.

When Gene Choy took over as club president, he had enough confidence in me to appoint me chairman of the special activities committee. I was surprised to find that all of the other five members of the committee were older than I. In Japan a committee chairmanship would be reserved for the oldest or most experienced member. Choy told me he would like my committee to undertake some social programs in which members and their wives would have an opportunity to get better acquainted with one another.

I jotted down some ideas and invited the committee members to my home for dinner after which we could discuss our projects. My wife, Renko, was happy to prepare a

Japanese meal, which wasn't too exotic, and my friends thought it was a delightful experience. When I was stationed in New York, Renko was tied down by our two young children and had little opportunity to get out into the community. In Los Angeles she was as determined as I to take part in the various activities, and her help, as in the dinner for the Lions, was invaluable.

At the end of the meeting one of the Lions, Bill Downs, invited the rest of us to dinner at his home for the next month's meeting. Bill sent us a written invitation as a reminder and I was surprised to see it was addressed to "Mr. and Mrs. Sogo."

"I've made a terrible mistake," I said to my wife. "I forgot that in America, unlike Japan, wives are usually invited together with their husbands to nonbusiness dinners."

Sure enough, all the wives, including mine, were with their husbands when we went to Bill Downs' home, and I was subjected to some gentle teasing for being a male chauvinist for having had a men-only dinner at my home. I had to smile through my embarrassment. I was learning to understand American culture through my mistakes.

In the late summer of 1975 it was announced that the Japanese imperial couple would visit Los Angeles on October 8. This inspired an idea for a "Japan Night" for the Lions. Of course, Emperor Hirohito and Empress Nagako had a very heavy schedule involving city officials and civic dignitaries, and our Lions club had no possible chance of becoming involved directly. My idea was to hold a Japanese cultural program for the Lions the evening before the emperor's arrival to take advantage of the wide interest in the imperial visit.

Gene Choy agreed it was a fine idea. He was even more pleased when I said I could justify the program as a JETRO public relations project and would underwrite all expenses. Thus the income from the tickets, 200 to be sold for $7 each, would go to the club's charitable activities fund.

My first task was to find a suitable program. I had heard that the Japanese government had produced a documentary film on the imperial family and the traditions surrounding it. The film was to be used as a public relations vehicle for their visit to various parts of the United States. There would be no better place to show it than the Lions' Japan Night.

But when I asked the Japanese consulate general in Los Angeles to loan me a copy, I received a flat turndown. When I demanded to know why, I was told that the imperial visit was several weeks in the future and they could not commit the film because they might receive other requests for it.

"Do you have it committed for that night?" I asked.

He did not. He just didn't want to let me have it.

I told him to forget it and went off in a huff. Then I sent a message to JETRO Tokyo asking that a copy of the film be purchased for me at the Foreign Ministry.

Several days later, JETRO Tokyo responded by asking about the nature of the Japan Night I was planning and for a list of the most prominent guests. "Damn bureaucrats," I thought. I was so upset I ordered one of my staff to tell Tokyo to forget the whole thing. Being more diplomatic than his boss, he managed somehow to placate JETRO's head office and get a copy of the film.

In Los Angeles I persuaded Shiseido, the cosmetics company; Suntory, which exported whiskey; and Noritake, the chinaware manufacturers, to donate door prizes. These were nice gifts but I wanted everyone to take home some memento of the evening. The solution was Japanese-made "Lion" brand toothbrush/toothpaste packets, which I bought as table favors. They stirred up much favorable comment among the Lions and their guests.

Jack Crowley, the master of ceremonies, scheduled me for the opening remarks. "I want you to speak in Japanese, a few sentences at a time," he said, "and I'll pretend I'm interpreting for you."

I spoke a few words, then stopped and looked at Jack. "Ladies and gentlemen," he said, "thank you very much for joining us in this Japan Night program." He was right so far. I said a few more sentences, and Jack repeated in English what he thought I had said. By then some of the audience had caught on to what was going on, so after Jack's next interpretation I said in English, "Thank you, Jack, but what I really said was..."

There was laughter and the evening was off to a great start.

The film and the rest of the program were received enthusiastically, and the Lions and their wives and friends—200 in all—left with a new understanding of Japan. Undoubtedly the program did not add or subtract a single dollar in the balance of trade, but I was confident that the effort had more than paid off in goodwill.

The success of Japan Night emboldened me to volunteer for another project totally unrelated to Japan. One day the directors of the Lions were searching for an interesting project that would help erase the club deficit, and not getting anywhere, when an idea came to me.

"How about a garage sale?" I asked.

There was no show of enthusiasm around the room.

"Let me explain," I said. "Before coming to Los Angeles, my family lived in a tiny Tokyo apartment in a four-story building for JETRO employees. I did not have a car and of course there was no garage. I don't think I will ever be able to own a house with a garage, like the one I live in now, in Japan. So I am intrigued by the idea of a garage sale. I would like to take part in one before returning to Japan. It may not be profitable, but it would provide an opportunity for getting together and I think it could be fun. And I would be happy to volunteer to organize it."

Actually, the Los Angeles Lions Club's very first garage sale did not require much organizing. I found that garage sales are so much a part of the American way of life that everyone knew what to do without being assigned a job. One couple offered the use of their garage. Others rummaged through attics for a variety of usable merchandise like old golf shoes, skis that were no longer used, outgrown clothing, books, and knick-knacks. Everyone took part in pricing the merchandise. Others made and put up posters advertising the sale. On the big day a large number of Lions and their wives came to socialize, if not to buy.

Our profit was $620. Some Japanese would sniff at the idea of involving the time and effort of a large number of people to make such a paltry sum. In Japan, more than likely some prominent and influential person would call on a wealthy member of the community and ask for a donation to erase the deficit.

What the Lions gained from the project was an opportunity to cooperate in a common goal, and that to me was far more valuable than the money that resulted. Our experience was a demonstration of commitment, which means more than simply giving money. It is something many Japanese have yet to understand.

Of course this is a generalization, and like all generalizations it is not entirely accurate, as demonstrated by my experience with Hanae Mori, the renowned fashion designer. My venture into her field, about which I knew nothing, began with a call from Keiichi Tachibana, Japan's consul general in Los Angeles.

He explained that he had been visited by representatives of a women's organization called the Gold Diggers who sponsored a fashion show each year to raise funds for disabled children. They had come to ask for help in getting the cooperation of some prominent Japanese designer and organizing a show. The consul general said that fashion shows were somewhat out of his field and he wanted to know what JETRO could do.

I had neither knowledge of nor interest in fashions, and nothing in my budget to support such a project. But it looked like a great way to promote goodwill, to participate in an important community function, and to promote the Japanese fashion and textile industry. I agreed to meet the women and learn more.

When they arrived at my office, I confessed my ignorance but expressed my desire to cooperate. "Do you have any particular designer in mind?" I asked.

"Hanae Mori," the ladies responded as one.

I recognized the name. She was not only Japanese, but one of the world's best-known designers. "Wow," I said to myself, "these ladies want to go first-class."

I explained to my visitors that my office had no budget for organizing fashion shows but promised to try to persuade JETRO in Tokyo that this was a project worthy of support. Somewhat to my surprise, Tokyo agreed and located Miss Mori's New York address. By coincidence I was scheduled to go to New York for the annual conference of Japanese businessmen in the U.S. with Japanese diplomats stationed in this country. I made an appointment to see her.

Hanae Mori was enthusiastic about presenting a show in Los Angeles, which she saw as the nation's western fashion capital. I explained that this was to be a charity event and confessed with some embarrassment that JETRO had limited funds. She said she would pay her own expenses, but asked that JETRO pay the expenses for a music director and three models from Japan. The date was set for November 3, 1975 at the Beverly Hilton in Beverly Hills.

In the next few months I received a first-class education about fashion shows, fund-raising, and working with strong-minded women. The primary lesson was to stay out of their way.

The Gold Diggers took care of everything from printing and sending out invitations to public relations and table decorations. Press International produced the programs without charge. Japan Air Lines was persuaded to donate tickets for the music director and the models. I was afraid the cost of stage decorations would be staggering, but Hanae Mori asked that the walls and floor of the stage be covered only with plain white cloth with just her name in large, black, stylized letters on the back wall. Even so, the expenses were larger than JETRO's public relations budget could stand. I took a deep breath and did what would have outraged the bean counters in Tokyo—I diverted funds from the out-of-town travel budget to the fashion show, confident that it would be so successful that no one would mind.

Hanae Mori Fashion Show in Los Angeles held by the request of Gold Diggers (November 3, 1975), a group that was raising funds to help disabled children. The show was a great success.

The Gold Diggers had set up 100 tables with ten places at each. All were sold except for one table reserved for some of the husbands of board members and me. The buzz of conversation died down as the show started with music. I had asked Hanae Mori several times if she needed an announcer or master of ceremonies. Each time she said no, and I finally understood why. The fashions did the talking. Eloquently. As the show ended with a bridal gown, Hanae Mori came on stage, slim, smiling, and striking. Everyone in the audience rose in tribute. To thunderous applause a young African-American boy in a wheelchair presented her with a bouquet of flowers.

I was overwhelmed with the realization that where grace, beauty and artistry were involved, there were no barriers between East and West, Japan and America. In a sense it might be said that Hanae Mori's fashion show displaying her designs with Japanese fabrics was little different from a show of Honda or Toyota cars, or Sony or Matsushita television sets, or other Japanese wares. But there was a significant difference. Americans had taken the initiative to introduce Hanae Mori's products to an American audience because they had the potential for enriching Americans' lives. Americans had paid good money for a charity, it is true, but they had attended because they wanted to see Hanae Mori's creations. There was no hard sell, but the event was the essence of good public relations. I hoped Tokyo would understand what a triumph this event was.

The euphoria of the moment returned some weeks later when Jack Whitehouse told me the fashion show was the best public relations project that any Japanese organization had sponsored in Los Angeles.

Chapter 9

The Triumphs and Frustrations of Education

JAPANESE BUSINESSMEN ARE KEENLY AWARE of the importance of education, but not often do they become involved in the schooling of their own children. This is regarded as the mother's responsibility. She tutors her offspring, helps them with homework, and urges them to study hard and get good grades so they can win entrance to the best secondary schools, and in turn be accepted by the best universities. Graduation from a top university is virtual assurance of a successful career. There is a Japanese expression—*Kyoiku Mama*—which means "Education Mama," to describe women who zealously, perhaps overzealously, promote the education of their children.

When Japanese businessmen are given overseas assignments, their children of high school age are often left with relatives so that their education can proceed without interruption, improving their chances of being accepted by a prestigious university. Younger children accompany their parents and attend the local schools. When I was assigned to Los Angeles, I was accompanied by my wife, Renko, and our two daughters, Naoko, thirteen, and Masako, twelve. Because of my wife's limited English I took the responsibility of enrolling our children in the public schools, which gave me an opportunity to see what the education system was like. Naoko was accepted as a seventh grader at South Pasadena Middle School, and Masako as a sixth grader at Monterey Hills Elementary School.

Naturally my wife and I were very apprehensive about how our children would fare. They understood hardly a word of English and now they were being thrown in among strangers whose customs were unfamiliar. Would they be able to make the necessary adjustments?

We needn't have worried. When I took Naoko to school for the first time, we were greeted warmly by a teacher and two other Japanese pupils enrolled at the school. They were the children of Japanese businessmen and had been in Los Angeles long enough to speak English and become familiar with school routine. They treated Naoko as an old friend and accepted the responsibility of looking after her until she was familiar with every aspect of school life.

At the elementary school the teachers went out of their way to help Masako adjust. For example, when the pupils studied arithmetic (with which Masako was familiar), she was taken to a kindergarten class where she was exposed to elementary English lessons. When students were assigned to write a report on some foreign country, Masako was told she could pick Japan and write the paper in Japanese, which I then checked over.

The kindness and thoughtfulness of the teachers amazed my wife and me. We asked around, and our Japanese friends reported that their children also were getting the same kind of treatment. Perhaps Americans took such caring for granted, but as a foreigner and guest in the United States, I was surprised and grateful and wondered what I could do to show my appreciation. That opportunity came one day in January 1975 in the form of a telephone call from Toshimitsu Furutani, deputy director of JETRO's Overseas Public Relations Department in Tokyo.

He told me $6,000 had been discovered unexpectedly in the funds available to his department. (I didn't ask why, although when I was in the department, we always ran short of funds.) JETRO's parent agency, MITI, had approved putting the $6,000 in a reserve fund, but then reversed itself unexpectedly and announced the money would be repossessed unless it was spent before the end of the fiscal year. This was less than three months away. Furutani said it would be easy to spend the money on any old project, but the difficulty was finding a worthy one that could be fully justified. He went on to say that he was canvassing a number of overseas JETRO offices in search of proposals and asked me if I had any bright ideas.

I could have put $6,000 to good use in the Los Angeles operating budget, but of course this wasn't what Furutani had in mind. "Give me a few days to refine an idea I've been playing with," I told him. "I think it is important to use the funds for a single important project, and not parcel out small amounts to a number of them."

The next day, I went to see Tadayuki Maeda, resident manager of the giant C. Itoh (now Itoh-chu) trading corporation, who was then president of the Japan Business Association of Southern California (JBASC) which had about 300 corporate members.

I began our conversation by reminding him of the extraordinarily warm way children of Japanese businessmen had been welcomed in the public schools, the sincere interest teachers had taken in them, and the feeling of many parents that something should be done to express their appreciation.

"As you know, this is an ongoing matter," I said. "All of us are rotated back to Japan after a few years. Just about the time the children have become fluent in English and adjusted to American schools, they leave. They are replaced by other Japanese children unfamiliar with the U.S., but the teachers are very patient about working with them. We have talked about ways of expressing our appreciation but haven't come up with an appropriate idea. Now I think I have one."

I pointed out that most American teachers probably never would have an opportunity to visit Japan. But, I said, they had demonstrated their interest in Japanese children and there would be no greater gift of appreciation than an expense-paid trip to Japan where, in addition to sightseeing, they could learn about Japanese culture and values.

Maeda listened quietly but I detected an interest. I went on: "What I am proposing is that JBASC set up a program to give one or two teachers an opportunity to visit Japan each summer. This will not be inexpensive, but we have 300 corporate members, and that should be enough to raise the necessary funds. At the moment I cannot make a promise, but if JBASC adopts the idea, I think I know how to get $6,000 to get the program under way."

Maeda smiled approval. "Please come to our next directors' meeting," he said.

Maeda opened the meeting in what I thought was a strange way: he said he was proposing an increase in the annual dues. "I have been president of this organization for almost a year," he stated, "and my duties have been concerned mostly with turning down requests for donations from various American organizations and supervising the Saturday Japanese-language school for our children. It is time that we should do more for the community, and that will require money."

I could see where Maeda was going.

One director interrupted him: "The latest financial report shows that the organization is comfortably in the black. Why should we raise the dues when we have no program for the community?"

Maeda turned to me and asked me to review our earlier conversation. I presented the idea of offering Los Angeles public school teachers an educational trip to Japan, and despite early skepticism it caught on. I had been thinking of a modest beginning, with one or two teachers to be rewarded each year. The JBASC voted in trips for ten, provided I could persuade JETRO to give the project the $6,000.

My friend Furutani in Tokyo embraced the idea warmly, but now came the task of working out the details. I turned to Jack Whitehouse for help. In Japan the proper approach would have been to ask the Board of Education to administer the plan and select teachers for the trip, and

I presumed this was the route we should take. Jack vetoed the proposal. "The Board of Education is a political group and its decisions usually are political," he said. "There is no assurance that the teachers selected for the trip would be most deserving from the Japanese point of view. If you want to make this a classroom-level program," he suggested, "we should make a list of elementary and middle schools in Los Angeles hosting children from Japan, then ask each principal to nominate the most deserving teacher from his or her faculty. Then a committee from the JBASC would make the final decision."

Eventually nine teachers were selected for the first "U.S. Teachers to Japan" program. JETRO made all the arrangements, including transportation and all the activities in Japan. In addition to the usual sightseeing and cultural tours, the program included a reunion with former pupils and an overnight stay in a Japanese home.

Later, in an evaluation of the program, the teachers reported that the homestay, although it was for only one night, was the most interesting part of the trip. But for the Japanese, arranging homestays was the most difficult part of the program. This may seem odd to middle-class Americans, who usually have a spare bedroom for guests. By contrast, Japanese homes are small, and at night in many households the living room furniture is pushed into a corner and bedding is spread on the floor. Many families who were asked to host the teachers had never had a foreigner in their home, much less had one stay the night. Understandably, they were reluctant to open their homes to overnight guests.

Finally, in desperation, a few JETRO employees who had lived overseas were asked to open their homes. But even some of them suffered from stress. I learned later that the wife of one JETRO employee had to take to her bed with nervous exhaustion after her guest departed. What most of the Japanese did not understand was that their American guests thought the crowded homes and rather ordinary meals were a novel and delightful experience.

The initial program was so successful that the idea soon spread. Before long, Japanese firms in various parts of the country were providing opportunities to visit Japan for teachers in Chicago, Detroit, Houston, Dallas, San Francisco, Atlanta, and Denver. The program spread to Canada in 1993 and to Great Britain in 1994. In Los Angeles the program had expanded so greatly that on its 20th anniversary in 1994, forty-nine educators and spouses were invited to Japan.

The interest that educators were showing in Japan encouraged more and more Japanese parents to visit American schools and take part in parent-teacher activities. But I perceived two problems that trouble me to this day.

The first is that what started out as an opportunity for classroom teachers—usually of limited means—to visit Japan was changed to a program for U.S. "educators," who usually turned out to be administrators. I think getting administrators involved is a fine idea but their inclusion reduced the number of opportunities for classroom teachers, the ones in direct contact with Japanese children. Perhaps there is need for a separate program for educators who are not classroom teachers.

The second is that, although the teacher visit idea was initiated by representatives of business firms, the Japanese as individuals have failed to support the program. It has become an official JETRO project, with JETRO employees making all the arrangements for meals, housing, and tours, and providing escorts for travel. Although it is usually the local Japan Business Associations that bear the greatest part of the program cost, JETRO has become their agent and there is little direct participation by companies, individual businesspeople, or families, except at welcome parties and farewell dinners. What started as a grassroots expression of appreciation and friendship has become just another project, and that's a pity.

Be that as it may, the kindness of American teachers and the personal interest they took in their pupils made schooling in the United States a wonderful experience for our children. But when we returned to Japan, we were to encounter unexpected and infuriating problems.

My assignment in Los Angeles ended on June 30, 1977, after nearly three years of interesting and, I hope, productive work. On that day my wife, Renko, and I and our two children left for Tokyo, crossed the international dateline, and landed at Haneda Airport the following day. Masako, our younger daughter, had finished eighth grade at South Pasadena Middle School a few days earlier. Naoko, our older daughter, had been graduated from the same school and was looking forward to entering high school in Japan. What she found was a mess of bureaucratic red tape and insensitive bureaucrats who made our homecoming anything but pleasant.

Naoko's continued education was much on our minds when we arrived in Japan. We learned quickly that Oizumi Kosha, an experimental school attached to the national Tokyo Gakugei University, had a special program for children like Naoko returning to Japan after a period abroad. A special entrance examination was to be held July 12, but the application had to be filed by July 4. I put everything aside to get the necessary documents and certification and submitted her application just before the deadline. In return I received a document certifying that she was entitled to take the entrance examination.

This proved to be false. She was not permitted to take the examination because, I was told, under further examination it was found she was not qualified under Ministry of Education rules.

Why? What were the rules?

The regulations, it was pointed out, required an applicant to have been graduated from a foreign junior high school by March 31 of the year the child applied for enrollment at a Japanese high school. Why March 31? This was the end of the school year in Japan. But the American school year ended in June, and that was when students, including Naoko, were graduated.

I eventually figured out that the purpose of the regulation was to accept only students who had been enrolled previously in foreign high schools. In other words, the student had to have been a tenth grader to be accepted into the tenth grade of Oizumi Kosha, and Naoko did not qualify because she had completed only the ninth grade by the time of the March deadline.

"Well," I asked, "why can't she be accepted as a ninth grader in your middle school?"

"That would not be possible", I was told, "because she is already a graduate of a middle school."

What a bureaucratic mess. I could sympathize with American and other foreign businessmen who ran into similar red tape in trying to do business under Japanese regulations.

The Oizumi Kosha administrator was sympathetic, but made it clear his hands were tied because the school was funded by the national government. Then he suggested I take Naoko to a private girls' academy where she could study until she became eligible to enter Oizumi Kosha the next year. The cost was enormous, but Naoko liked the school and I was relieved that she would not have to waste a year.

My experience with the red tape continued to rankle me, however. The regulation seemed so unnecessary and a burden on families whose work took them overseas. One day I telephoned the Ministry of Education and asked to speak with someone in the department responsible for elementary and middle schools. I related my experience to the man who answered the telephone and asked him to explain the regulations governing such cases.

"Hold on a moment," he said. It turned out to be a long moment. Eventually he returned and said, "This section is not in charge of such matters. Please call...." and he referred me to another department.

I recognized the bureaucratic tactic, when one wasn't sure what to do, of denying responsibility and passing the buck to someone else. Certainly persons who had come to

JETRO for information or assistance had run into the same kind of treatment, and I had fought to prevent it.

Angrily, I said: "You know as well as I do that the Ministry of Education is one entity, and I will not tolerate being passed around from department to department without getting answers. There must be a simple answer to my question. If you cannot give me the information I seek about a silly regulation that may have changed the course of my daughter's life, and which affects hundreds of other Japanese children returning home from overseas, I am prepared to take legal action against the Ministry of Education and demand return of my application fee. That might be the best way to inform the public about your unfair regulation."

He must have turned away from the phone because I heard him say to a colleague: "What shall we do with this man? He is angry and says that he is going to sue us."

I hung up in utter frustration. I did not file suit as I had threatened—that would have been most un-Japanese of me—but lost no opportunity to mention the problem to friends in the mass media. My concern was for the hundreds of Japanese children returning with their families from overseas assignments who faced unfair treatment for no logical reason. What particularly rankled me was the contrast between the warm and helpful assistance my children received in the United States and the rigid, unnecessary restrictions they faced on return to their home country.

There must have been others who complained. Over the years the problem has largely been alleviated.

Chapter 10

Searching for Understanding

My new assignment in Tokyo was as director of the entire Overseas Public Relations Department. I was familiar with the routine. I seemed to be hurrying from meeting to meeting to lunches and receptions with no real opportunity to accomplish anything useful. What I missed most, I realized, was the opportunity to participate in extracurricular activities, as I had done in Los Angeles.

I realized anew that Japanese society neither approved of nor appreciated volunteerism. An employee was expected to spend his or her time and energy only on activities that would profit the company directly. A volunteer was regarded as someone with nothing much else to do.

Oddly enough, it was rising tension over trade imbalance between the United States and Japan, which was of great concern to JETRO, that opened the way to a useful voluntary activity. Japan's trade surplus with the United States was soaring, to the dismay of leaders of both countries. It was $7.3 billion in 1977, and the momentum was to continue to $10.1 billion in 1978 and then $6 billion in 1979.

From Tokyo's point of view, Japan had been trying very hard to bring trade into balance. In 1968, Japan averted a critical confrontation with the United States by introducing "voluntary" restriction of steel shipments. The restrictions were extended to textiles in 1972. The next issue was color television sets; Japan "voluntarily" cut back exports in 1977 to 60 percent of the previous year's export total. Eventually, these restrictions led Japanese manufacturers of television sets, automobiles, computers, and computer chips to open plants in the United States and build their products with American labor.

I had been back in Tokyo only a month in 1977 when a high MITI official named Hiroshi Kawasaki asked me to come to his office. A summons from MITI usually meant bad news, but Kawasaki was quite congenial.

Some directors of the American Chamber of Commerce in Japan (ACCJ) had come to him, he said, and asked for help in raising private funds for a group to seek betterment of U.S.-Japanese relations, specifically to see what could be done to promote the import of American products to Japan and try to bring trade more into balance. Mr. Kawasaki asked what I thought of the idea.

I replied that although I didn't know what the Americans had in mind, the proposal held promise if both Japanese and Americans at the grassroots of trade would become involved. I offered to help keep expenses down by providing JETRO's conference rooms for meetings and using JETRO as a secretariat.

"But before we go any further," I said, "there should be a clear understanding. The organization should not be used by

Americans simply as a forum for accusing Japan of having a closed market or for the Japanese to refute that charge. Membership should be open to anyone who wants to contribute to improvement of relations between the two countries, and they should join as individuals and not as representatives of particular companies. I would like to see open discussion of the many problems we face, with cooperative action to try to improve the situation."

Kawasaki nodded agreement. Two weeks later the first meeting was held with a core group of Japanese and Americans. We decided to call our organization the U.S.-Japan Trade Study Group, or TSG for short.

I had wanted interested persons to take part as individuals, but perhaps it was inevitable that the initial Japanese participants were representatives of the various

THE FIRST MEETING OF THE U.S.–JAPAN TRADE STUDY GROUP (TSG) WAS HELD AUGUST 23, 1977, AT JETRO'S EXECUTIVE CONFERENCE ROOM.

organizations MITI had contacted about joining: Keidanren (Federation of Economic Organizations), the Foreign Trade Council of Japan, the Japan Chamber of Commerce and Industry, the U.S.-Japan Economic Council. So far as I could tell, the members of ACCJ who attended the first meeting came as individuals, although the U.S. Embassy was represented. A total of twenty-one men joined the first meeting but before long the membership approached 100.

Of course any organization must have officers. Dick Yamashita and I were elected cochairmen. Dick was an American of Japanese ancestry and president of Marcom International, involved with the computer industry and communication. His American viewpoint plus knowledge of Japanese psychology and language made him particularly valuable. We took turns chairing the meetings.

The language problem illustrates the difficulty Japanese and Americans have in communicating. Most of the Americans spoke no Japanese, and because almost all the Japanese could understood both languages, our meetings were held in English. But even though the Japanese knew English, they found it difficult to carry on a debate or argue a complex point in English, and too often they found it more comfortable to remain silent. Thus we had to have an interpreter on hand. But some Americans, knowing that most of the Japanese understood English, became frustrated by the long interpretations and would stop participating in discussions for a while.

At the time, the focus of American complaints about the Japanese trade surplus was something referred to as

Japan's non-tariff barriers (NTB). Hardly a day passed without NTB being mentioned in the newspapers. I am not sure that anyone understood the nature of an NTB. A news story might report that "Japan's complicated distribution system is a critical non-tariff barrier," but there were no suggestions as to how a basic and traditional distribution system that had served Japan well over the centuries should be changed to accommodate Americans. It was obvious that NTB, whatever it was, frustrated Americans, but even with my JETRO background I could not understand what the complaint was about or what could be done about it. Many Japanese were inclined to protest that Americans were using NTB as a straw man to blame for inept, uninformed, and lackadaisical efforts to penetrate the Japanese market.

Obviously this could be, or perhaps already was, an inflammatory issue, and TSG picked it as a subject for investigation. Americans and Japanese working together set out to learn if there were any Japanese laws, regulations, or even cultural customs blocking entry of American products and services into the Japanese market. The objective was to identify the so-called non-tariff barriers and try to do something about them if they existed and appeared to be unfair.

It was quickly discovered that TSG had taken on an enormous task that should be broken down into subdivisions that could be managed by volunteers. One group took on problems with standards, government inspection and certification systems, the use of "marks" of approval, customs classifications, quota administration, customs valuation and clearance procedures, financing problems, and government-procurement practices.

Another committee was put in charge of studying and analyzing the marketability of specific products and services with particular attention to any visible or invisible trade barriers. Seven special task forces were established to study problems with electrical appliances, automobiles, forestry products, agricultural chemicals, processed foods, health care products, and trade finance, which demonstrates the complexity of trade problems. When these various committees began working, each chairman reported findings at TSG's monthly meetings. These reports were followed by lively comments and discussion that stimulated further comment. Frequently we invited outside speakers, such as a MITI official in charge of electrical appliances or private or government visitors from the United States.

About a year after TSG was formed, Dick Yamashita asked me to come to the U.S. Embassy to meet members of the U.S.-Japan Trade Task Force of the House Ways and Means Committee. Congressmen James Jones of Oklahoma, the chairman, and Bill Frenzel of Minnesota were there with TSG members Faneuil Adams Jr., Jim Baloun, and Yamashita. Members of TSG took turns explaining our organization's activities.

Congressman Jones seemed to be impressed and did what any American politician would do. He lauded TSG's goals and offered federal funds to support the program.

Fan Adams, president of the Mobil Oil company's operations in Japan, said quickly: "Sir, we don't need any federal funding. If we receive money from the U.S. government, the Japanese will assume we are working for the government, just as Americans would believe we were propagandists for the Japanese if we accepted funding from the Japanese government.

"Please understand that the goals of this group are to identify possible obstacles to the healthy growth of U.S.-Japan trade and to find ways to correct the problems. In order to establish trust on both sides, we need to be neutral and independent. When we need money, we will raise it ourselves."

This was my first experience meeting face-to-face with a member of Congress and I was struck by the openness and frankness of the discussion. In Japan there is a superior/subordinate relationship between politicians and voters. Politicians are called *Sensei,* meaning "master" or "teacher." There was no such relationship between these American businessmen and their representatives in Congress. The businessmen were telling the congressmen exactly what they thought and the congressmen listened carefully. It was an eye-opening experience.

The congressmen were invited to the TSG monthly meeting that afternoon. So many members showed up that we had to move to a larger conference room. If anyone expected an extraordinary meeting, he was disappointed. At the end, I as chairman invited the congressmen to offer a few comments about their mission.

Congressman Jones noted wryly that nothing was happening on the official level to improve the U.S.-Japanese trade situation, saying it was like a baseball game with no score, no runners on base, no hits, and no errors. Later, P.M.G. Clarke, chairman of the TSG electrical appliance task force, told Congressman Jones he was wrong. MITI, working with his group, was trying to modify regulations on imported electrical appliances.

Several months later, Congressman Jones submitted to Congress the so-called Jones Report, strongly criticizing Japan's trade policies. It was widely read by Japanese government officials—perhaps more closely in Tokyo than in Washington. I was pleased to see that Congressman Jones mentioned TSG's efforts and recognized it as a group that both governments could listen to.

Congressman Jones returned to Japan again early in 1980 with two other members of the House trade subcommittee. Some members of the TSG taskforce met with him to report our progress, and he promised it would be given proper attention.

By the spring of 1980 the TSG's various committees were far enough along in their study of so-called non-tariff barriers that we could consider publishing a summary, to be called "The Special Progress Report." Committee members submitted reports that were in turn submitted to others for review. Even in a city as large as Tokyo, space where we could meet after working hours was difficult to find. The large corporations had tight security rules and were unwilling to open their doors to nonemployees at night. Hotel space was too expensive and coffeehouses were too noisy. Fan Adams came to our rescue by opening his home for the meetings, where the final version was put together. The fact that we planned to publish the report in two languages made our task all the more daunting.

One night Adams had a disturbing thought: "If we are to print this document and distribute it to government agencies, among others, we must be absolutely sure that everything in it is accurate. An inaccuracy, especially about regulations, will not only discredit the report and TSG, but it would be unfair to the agencies concerned." Adams suggested a draft be shown to the various government departments involved and the information verified, and none of us could argue with him.

Five government ministries were involved. Taxes, trade financing, and automobile tax issues came under the Ministry of Finance. Electrical appliances, quality marks, and product testing involved the Ministry of International Trade and Industry. Forestry products and processed food were under the Ministry of Agriculture and Forestry. Vehicle registration and imported cars were overseen by the Ministry of Transportation. Safety standards, food sanitation, and inspection were in the purview of the Ministry of Health and Welfare.

Most of the reports had been researched and written by volunteers on their own time. But the government ministries would have to be visited during regular business hours, and our volunteers were reluctant to spend what might turn out to be endless hours with the bureaucrats. In addition, unlike the U.S. where government and business can talk as equals, all corporations in Japan operate under close government supervision, and going to see a bureaucrat on a matter not directly related to company business posed an uncomfortable situation. So who would take the time and make the effort to meet with a variety of bureaucrats? I felt all eyes on me. I agreed to have our report checked. After all, I was a JETRO bureaucrat, cochairman of TSG, and was convinced the report was an extremely valuable document.

I ran into unexpected luck. Two of the ministries had senior officials working at JETRO on temporary assignment, and it was natural for them to be helpful. They directed me to the proper persons at the Ministry of Finance and Ministry of Agriculture and Forestry with assurances that I would find cooperation in reviewing the report. And because a representative of the Ministry of International Trade and Industry was on our committee, I did not have to go there.

That left the Ministries of Transportation and of Health and Welfare. The Transportation official was accommodating and assured me that the draft would be reviewed without delay. The interview lasted only ten minutes.

At the Ministry of Health and Welfare, a committee of seven grim-faced bureaucrats received me. They listened in silence as I explained TSG, its purpose, and the report. I had barely concluded when one of the bureaucrats asked with a sneer, "Since when did JETRO become an agent of the United States?"

I tried to remain calm because I needed the ministry's cooperation. "JETRO is my employer," I explained, "but JETRO has nothing to do with TSG and this report. It is the work solely of volunteers concerned with improving understanding between Japan and the United States. If we were an agent of the United States, why would I be here asking you to review the document before publishing it?"

Another man broke in: "Trade negotiations are being conducted by the two governments. Why does a group of volunteers need to get involved?"

Before I could reply, still another man asked: "If you were in America, would you be asking U.S. officials to check a document written in Japanese? Remember, you are in Japan, and you have no right to expect us to comment on your English-language report."

He was right, of course. From the very beginning we had planned to have the report issued in Japanese as well as English, even though translation was expensive. But in the hurry to have the report published, I had visited the ministries before the original English was fully translated. I resented being humiliated, but left with their promise that they would review the Japanese-language version of that part of the report that applied to them. As I returned to my office I wondered whether the arrogance of Japanese officials might be an important trade barrier. Some of my non-Japanese friends had pointed out that in addition to strict regulations and complicated procedures, bureaucratic attitudes gave the impression that Japanese markets were closed. The officials at the Ministry of Health and Welfare knew that I was a senior JETRO official and, by reason of my position, was entitled to certain respect and courtesy. I had not expected bowing and scraping, but instead of showing common decency they had treated me rudely. It was not difficult to imagine the kind of reception a representative of a small foreign company would get if he or she went to the ministry with a problem.

Eventually TSG received assurance from the five ministries that the sections involving them were accurate. To make sure that the public understood that TSG alone was responsible for the report, the following passage was included in the publication:

> During the course of preparing this progress report, the TSG has asked individuals from various Japanese government agencies for verification of the contents as well as for advice. The TSG would like to take this opportunity to express its appreciation for their valuable input.... Not all the comments and suggestions made by them are included in this report. Therefore, the TSG would like to make it clear that the omission of some comments, for various reasons, from the report is not the responsibility of the individuals from the various Japanese government agencies as this is a TSG report and the contents do not reflect the official position of the Japanese government.

Eventually the report neared completion. But what would we do with it? Obviously it should be printed and distributed, but we had no funds. Once again Fan Adams, who represented Mobil Sekiyu (Petroleum), came to our rescue. He provided the funds to print 3,000 copies. The date for their distribution was set at April 21, 1980.

There were to be two press conferences to introduce the report, the first at JETRO's offices at 12:30 P.M. for Japanese members of the JETRO "press club." There are many such press clubs whose membership is limited to reporters who cover a specific organization or agency. In this case it was JETRO. A second briefing, in English, was scheduled for 2:30 P.M. for foreign correspondents and other journalists who were not members of the press club.

Much to our dismay, both briefings were sparsely attended. That morning, there had been rumors that the government was about to announce stiff economic sanctions against Iran, where militant students had seized the U.S. Embassy and disrupted the worldwide oil supply. The reporters were out tracking down that story. (Japan's economic sanctions were announced April 24.) Stories about the TSG report were carried in only two Japanese newspapers (*Japan Economic Journal, Tokyo Shimbun)* and two English-language papers (*Japan Times, Mainichi Daily News*). Both of the English-language stories were brief. *The Japan Times* headline read, "U.S. Firms Must Try Harder in Japan—Conclusion of Special Trade Report." The *Mainichi* headline was "U.S. Urged to Make More Effort—Trade Study Group Report."

If these headlines are a bit confusing, it's because the English-language press in Japan uses this style for attributing a statement. The more direct American style would have been to say, "U.S. Firms Must Try Harder in Japan, Joint Trade Report Urges" or "Joint Study Group Urges U.S. Firms to Push Trade Efforts."

Although the report attracted relatively little attention in Japan, it won considerable notice in American official circles. In what was called the second Jones Report, Congressman Jones discussed TSG in detail and included many quotations from our findings. He noted that TSG was slowly helping to solve trade problems, particularly in the field of standardization, and credited us with being an influential group. Congressman Sam Gibbons, chairman of the House trade subcommittee, who also had met with us on a visit to Japan, mentioned TSG prominently in his report. He noted that TSG was an organization dedicated to solving trade problems and that the per-dollar effect of the volunteer group's efforts was more significant than that of many official trade promotion programs.

We were pleased that although the TSG report received little public notice, it was given substantial official attention. As Japan's trade surplus continued to grow and the United States sought new ways to overcome what were identified as non-tariff barriers, the TSG report came to be regarded as a valuable source of information. I suppose one reason the report did not attract immediate public attention was the absence of a tantalizing title, something like "The Truth Behind the U.S.-Japan Economic War." But our work had not failed. It simply needed time to be appreciated.

I learned many lessons from the TSG experience. I learned that Americans and Japanese can work together beyond their individual interests if they trust each other and understand that they are cooperating for the common good rather than the selfish interests of their companies or countries. And I developed strong friendships with men who generously donated their time, knowledge, and experience toward the goal of understanding.

This message was expressed in part in the introduction to the printed report:

> We recognize that this trade imbalance has resulted more from the disparity between the efforts made by Japanese exporters to develop U.S. markets for their goods and the efforts made by U.S. companies to develop markets for their goods, than from any remaining Japanese non-tariff barriers. The Japanese government's positive attitude towards the export efforts of Japanese firms has contributed to this disparity. Any long-term improvement in the bilateral trade imbalance will depend more on improved performance by both U.S. business and government in promoting exports than on the removal of remaining Japanese non-tariff barriers. We also believe, however, that remaining non-tariff barriers in Japan are a contributing factor to the bilateral trade imbalance and act as a major irritant in U.S.-Japan economic relations.

If an American group had said this, it could be accused of Japan-bashing. If a Japanese group said it, it might be seen as just another lame excuse. But because this message came from a group like TSG in which both American and Japanese volunteers were working on a problem on an equal basis, it was bound to be noticed.

Participation in TSG was harder for the Japanese than for the Americans, and indeed they were less active. Most Japanese are good workers, trained to work hard for their company or organization, but they are less aware of the concept of volunteerism. In my own case, TSG's program complemented my work at JETRO, but I did not pretend TSG was an official project. I spent my own time in promoting its program. But still, many of those who knew of my involvement in TSG still consider it a JETRO project, or at least something organized by JETRO. In reality it was strictly a grassroots, voluntary effort by Japanese and Americans who realized a need and volunteered to meet it.

Chapter 11

A Columnist, Briefly

As Japan became a more important player on the world economic scene, an increasing number of foreigners visited the country. Many of them were dignitaries, such as government representatives, corporate executives, journalists, and academicians. Virtually all received the red carpet treatment, at which Japan excels, and I was involved in assisting and entertaining many of them.

One day it occurred to me that while JETRO was focusing its attention on these star guests, it was paying little attention to the growing number of businessmen and businesswomen living and working in Japan as representatives of foreign companies. I, and many other Japanese involved with foreigners, knew very little about them, other than those with whom we had daily contact, or people like members of TSG with whom we were involved in special projects.

I wondered what the other foreigners were thinking, how much they knew about Japan and Japanese culture, what they would like to see and know about the country that would create better understanding, and how JETRO could help them do a better job for their employers.

But how could we reach such people? Obviously the simplest way was through the locally published English-language newspapers. I called a meeting with editorial representatives of the *Japan Times*, *Yomiuri*, *Mainichi Daily News* and *Asahi Evening News*, told them of my concerns; and offered JETRO's cooperation in helping them to make Japan more interesting and understandable to residents from abroad. Everyone agreed something needed to be done, but nothing happened until one day when several men from the *Mainichi* came to my office to talk about a special edition featuring trade and industry. In the course of our conversation I mentioned my earlier meeting with newspaper editors and remarked, "I wonder whether foreigners subscribing to your newspaper, instead of reading about Japan all the time, wouldn't be interested in what an astute Japanese observer thinks about their countries." It was only a casual thought and I went on to other matters.

That evening the editor of the *Mainichi Daily News* called me and said he had heard about my idea of a feature in which Japanese would express frank views about Americans. I replied that we had talked about something like that. "Have you mentioned this idea to any other newspaper?" he asked.

"Well," I replied, "I guess I've talked about something like that to a number of papers, but no one seemed the least bit interested."

"Good," the editor said. "I like the idea and if you don't mind, I'd like to do something with it. Maybe a regular column in which the writer expresses some very frank opinions."

"That pleases me," I said. "I think it would be an effective feature if you could find the right person to write down his honest feelings about America and Americans. Good luck."

"No," he said. "I want you to write the column."

I was startled. "Oh, no, no," I protested. "I'm just proposing an idea. I had no intention of carrying it out myself. I'm very, very busy at the office and I am involved deeply with the Trade Study Group." And even if I had the time to write, I doubted that my ideas would interest anybody.

The editor wasn't the kind of man to take no for an answer. He called me twice more and I broke down to the point of asking for a little time to consider the proposal.

I kept turning over ideas for the column in my mind. One night, after reaching home about 9 P.M., which was about my usual time, I sat down to put some of my thoughts on paper. Writing in Japanese, I expressed some of the things I couldn't understand about America even though I had lived there, things I thought strange, and questions about why Americans did things a particular and seemingly illogical way. After writing for a while, I realized that I was simply putting down on paper matters that Japanese friends and I had discussed over meals or coffee in Los Angeles. I picked a single subject and before I knew it, I had what seemed to be an interesting draft.

The next day, I telephoned the editor and said I was wondering about details of his plan. He replied that he was thinking about at least seven articles, each about 2,000 words, to be published twice a week. He said if I wanted to write in Japanese, he would have the articles translated.

I replied that I was willing to accept his offer, but I wanted to have the entire series (which turned out to be twenty-four installments) written before publication started so that I wouldn't be worrying about deadlines. Thus began my brief but enjoyable career as a newspaper pundit.

My first column sought to introduce my objective by noting that though it was true that Japan had a large surplus in trade with the United States, the opposite was true in the matter of information. The Japanese must try harder to absorb knowledge about America and Americans, I wrote, and I said I would try to share with readers questions the Japanese had about the U.S. and try to answer them. I went on to say that some of my explanations might seem to be erroneous or inappropriate from the American point of view, but my intention was to explore different perceptions and not to judge right or wrong.

In due time my first column was turned in to the editor, and presently the English translation was returned for my approval. The English was correct and the translation was accurate. But I felt the finished product was not "me." This was understandable. The translator and I had never spoken to each other, and he or she had worked from sterile words on a printed page. I explained my concerns to the editor and received his approval to hire my own translator. The logical person for that job was George Kaye, an American consultant at Press International, He was fluent in Japanese and had translated many of my speeches.

Working nights and weekends, I finally completed seven essays with tentative titles like "Pardon Me for Saying So but Americans Don't Apologize Enough," "Tipping and Gratuities," and "American School Life as Seen by Japanese Parents and Children."

The series was to be called *The Other Side of the Twain*. It was a takeoff on a popular column titled *Never the Twain*... in the *Japan Times*, by my friend Don Maloney, introducing American views of Japan. Since my columns would focus on Japanese views of America and Americans, the title seemed apt. Quotations from my apology column indicate the approach I took:

> Fifteen years ago, when my transfer to an office in the United States was decided and I was about to go to America for the first time in my life, an older friend advised me: "When you arrive in the United States, forget the words 'I am sorry'."
>
> It's unfortunate because "I am sorry" is probably the easiest English expression for the Japanese to say. This is not simply because the words are easy to remember or pronounce. Rather, both in family life and in the business world in Japan, such expressions as "*Moshiwake-nai,*" "*Sumimasen*" and "*Shitsurei shimashita*" are all forms of apology and used every day. At times and in some situations these Japanese expressions have a nuance that cannot be fully translated into English, but in straining to do so—with what usually is translated as "I am sorry"—there are numerous pitfalls that one must avoid.

I naturally expected that this theme would be included when several persons in my Los Angelels office drew up an inventory on "the incomprehensibility of Americans according to Japanese standards". As one Japanese woman employee commented, "Americans just don't apologize."

Please don't misunderstand me. We had often heard the words "I am sorry," or "Excuse me" in the United States as well as from Americans residing in Japan. The real meaning of the woman employee's statement that "Americans just don't apologize" is that these words are not uttered by Americans when the Japanese would expect them to. Let me give you some examples.

1. Let us suppose that one day while you are driving, someone's car happens to bump into the rear of your car. If the driver of the other car is an American, you should never expect to hear the words "I am sorry." According to those in the know, to say "I am sorry" is an admission of guilt and could be used by the other party as a basis for demanding a fabulous sum for compensation at some later date.

Therefore, this expression seems to be taboo in such situations in the United States. Americans ought to know, however, that in Japan a frank admission of one's error serves to increase other people's trust in one.

2. On the very day that I arrived in New York 15 years ago, a plane of an American airline crashed. One of the staff members of our New York office, who was aboard that plane, was a victim of that accident and died.

Neither on the following day nor on any day afterward did a "notice of apology" appear in the advertising columns of the newspapers. Having just arrived in the United States from Japan—in other words, still measuring things entirely with a Japanese "yardstick"—I thought this was quite peculiar. Since a plane had crashed and a large number of passengers had died, it would seem only natural for the airline to express its apologies to the families and friends of the victims and to the large number of Americans who had worried. Not only was an apology overlooked, but the president of the airline didn't even resign. In fact, no one resigned to take responsibility for the incident.

The foregoing two examples concern accidents involving human lives. There are many situations in everyday life when the Japanese expect one word of regret from Americans, and none is forthcoming. When someone is late for an appointment, it is not his own fault, but that of the "crazy traffic jam." If a product is not delivered on the promised day, the manufacturer is not to blame, rather it is because another company that should have delivered the materials was tardy.

In the eyes of the Japanese, there are too many instances when Americans go to great lengths to prove that they are absolutely right. If they want to get along better with the Japanese, I would recommend to my American friends that they use more freely the words "I am sorry."

On the other hand, I think I would like to introduce into Japan the American habit of instantly saying "I am sorry," "Excuse me," or "Pardon me" when shoulders brush in an elevator. It is in the American elevator that "*Shitsurei*"—which the Japanese have begun to forget—remains very much. At least to me, it shouldn't seem to be so difficult for

> Americans to transfer this "I am sorry" to the roads, companies and homes of their country."

Not all the columns were in this vein. In an essay on American school life I introduced things that seemed strange to Japanese parents and children, as seen through the observations of my younger daughter. For example, she noticed that when a teacher asked a question in class, almost everyone raised his or her hand to answer. And if a student gave a completely erroneous answer, his or her reaction would be not of embarrassment or frustration, but "Well, I almost got it."

In a similar situation in Japan, the student would be mortified that he or she had volunteered to answer a question and failed to do it correctly.

My daughter thought it was a fine idea that American schools hired janitors to clean the rooms whereas in Japan the students themselves took on that duty. But her parents took the point of view that cleaning a classroom was part of a child's education. Perhaps the attitude of the American children becomes understandable when, asked what they would like to become when they grew up, a large number said they wanted to be lawyers.

My first column ran on Tuesday, January 24, 1978. I had no idea what sort of reaction it would receive, but within a few days after publication of a column, the letters began to pour in to the newspaper. Most of them were angry. Some correspondents accused me of being the No. 1 Japanese superpatriot. Others found my writing vacuous, pompous, shallow, and haughty. On the matter of why Americans seemed to like filing lawsuits, one reader wrote me a long letter explaining the American judicial system.

When some of these letters were printed in the *Mainichi's* Readers' Forum, some of my friends expressed alarm. They feared I would react emotionally to having my views rejected, and urged me to stop the series. I explained that I had absolutely no intention of provoking or speaking ill of Americans, but was writing the way I was because I believed exchanges of honest opinions were essential to understanding. But it concerned me that so many readers did not see my point.

About a month after the series got under way, the *Mainichi* began publishing letters that came to my defense. One said:

> I am not a frequent contributor to readers' columns, but I feel that someone must speak in defense of Shinsaku Sogo. In recent weeks he has been sharply criticized, and a few of the criticisms made might be valid, but it is regrettable that Mr. Sogo's detractors have clearly misunderstood some of his statements, have argued from ethnocentrism and worst of all, have loaded their commentary with condescension and flippancy...the language of Mr. Sogo's critics is distressing and seems less a product of misunderstanding than of overreaction and perhaps even some unconscious prejudice.

That letter was the forerunner of a number of others whose authors saw merit in what I was writing. One letter urged residents of "Gaijin land" to come to my support. Another said: "I have clipped some of these articles and sent them to friends in the U.S. who have many Japanese guests. Mr. Sogo's gentle, witty explanations of differences between countries will undoubtedly smooth the way for daily living for persons fortunate enough to get to know the two countries."

At the very least my columns had provoked thought among non-Japanese living in my country, and I would like to think the result was worth the effort. The comment that amused me the most was that the "worst part" of my column was the last sentence: "To be continued."

The experience of sharing my thoughts with a broad audience confirmed my belief that in order to communicate with Americans, Japanese must speak out. Unless they did so, there would be little understanding. I believed that Americans would appreciate the effort. However, understanding did not necessarily mean agreement.

Another point is that Japanese often find it difficult to speak directly to a problem. They depend more on intuition, on the part of both sides of an issue, rather than direct language, to reach understanding, and this is something that both Japanese and Americans must learn to appreciate.

Although the distance between the United States and Japan has been shortened by communications technology, there is still a formidable understanding gap between the two peoples. When Japanese talk about communication with the United States, they tend to think of public relations activities by government and private industry. The most important element is the individual. But it is hard for Japanese to understand this point, and even harder to put the idea into practice.

My series provoked enough interest that the *Mainichi* wanted me to write a book-length manuscript that they would publish. That meant twenty more columns, which was more than I had time to attempt. I declined the invitation, saying the new friends and acquaintances I had made from the series were reward enough.

I had not expected to be paid for the writing, so I was surprised to receive an honorarium. Two days later, Press International sent me a bill for translation services. It was ¥6000 yen higher than what I had received from the newspaper. I think ¥6000 was a low price for the experience of being able to share my thoughts with a wide cross section of the public.

CHAPTER 12

FCC, the Young Ambassadors

BEING PUBLISHED IN THE *MAINICHI* LED TO AN INTERESTING and useful experience. It began one day when I received a call from an American named Bunny Cramer, who identified herself as cofounder and chairperson of a group called Forum for Corporate Communications (FCC). She said she had been reading my columns and asked if I would be interested in speaking to her group about international communications.

I observed that her organization had a formidable-sounding name, and she quickly assured me that it was a group of young Americans with only fifteen members. She said they met monthly and hoped to have a number of others in attendance if I would speak at one of their meetings.

Six years earlier, when I had hired Melinda Ewing as a part-time secretary and typist, it was rare for a Japanese firm to employ a foreigner. I was surprised to hear that there were enough young Americans working for Japanese firms in Tokyo to organize a club.

The stereotype of the American living in Tokyo had been a large, beefy man heading a multinational corporation, who spoke almost no Japanese, was housed in an expensive apartment where his wife had a maid, traveled to his office in a chauffeur-driven company car, collected Japanese art, and spent most of his leisure time sipping drinks and playing gin rummy at the American Club in Roppongi. He resided in Japan but lived in a separate world.

Members of FCC were of a different breed. Some had come to Japan originally as exchange students. Some had studied Japanese in college. Some were married to Japanese. They were young and ambitious, reasonably fluent in the Japanese-language, and were accustomed to living and working Japanese-style. The Japanese firms they worked for included large trading houses, a manufacturer, an advertising agency, and a public relations firm. But, I found, most of them were only part-time English specialists helping the Japanese staff to handle English-language correspondence and produce English-language brochures, press releases, and advertising copy.

Nearly thirty of them were at the meeting where I spoke. I titled my presentation "International Communication from a Japanese Viewpoint," but fortunately the talk was not as formal as the title would indicate. The gist of what I said was that Japanese had just begun to realize the importance of international communication, but were somewhat at a loss as to how it should be done. Although language was a barrier, cultural differences were at the root of the problem, I said.

As an example I cited a brochure titled "The Japanese Market: The Myth and the Reality," which the Ministry of

International Trade and Industry had published in English. Within days, one of Tokyo's English-language newspapers ran a highly critical letter from a reader suggesting it would be more appropriate to call the brochure "The Japanese Market: The Reality and the Myth," proof that the brochure had failed in its effort to communicate. I also told of the Electric Industries Association of Japan buying a two-page advertisement in the *New York Times* and the *Washington Post*. Under a headline reading "Open Letter to U.S. Congressmen," the advertisement considered unfair the American accusation that Japanese firms were dumping color television sets in the U.S. market. Almost immediately the president of a major U.S. TV manufacturer called a press conference to denounce the ad as an effort to confuse American consumers on the issue of Japan dumping its products. And of course the American retort was given prominent press coverage, which drew attention to the problem rather than ameliorating it.

The problem, I told the members of FCC, was that Japan was responding to the communication problem from the viewpoint of an industry, or of the government, whereas it probably would have been much more effective to attack problems of understanding on the individual level. But in the Japanese culture, I pointed out, there is subtle pressure to deter individuals from taking the initiative on any matter, leaving decisions and actions to the group, the industry, or the government. There would not be true communication between Japan and America until individual Japanese learned to communicate with individual Americans. I concluded by asking the members of FCC to help me understand their culture so that I could better contribute to their understanding of Japan.

All of that must have made an impression because I was warmly welcomed when I asked, somewhat hesitantly, whether I could become a member of FCC. Thus began an interesting—and useful—experience.

Space is always a problem in Japan and I was able to help FCC in this regard. Because virtually all the members lived in tiny apartments, meetings even of small committees in their homes were out of the question. Being very junior employees of their companies, members of FCC could not consider asking for after-hours use of company conference rooms. Coffeehouses were noisy and expensive in that guests felt obliged to continue reordering in order to keep their tables. So they took up my offer and made the International Lounge at JETRO their meeting place for evening workshops and monthly board sessions. I don't think any of the members realized that when the meeting was over, I emptied the ashtrays, turned off the lights, locked the door and returned the key to the guard.

The informal, spontaneous camaraderie of the young Americans, so different from the seriousness with which young Japanese went about their way, was a delight. Monthly dinner meetings featuring a prominent speaker (Ambassador Mike Mansfield and former prime minister Takeo Fukuda, among others) were held at the Foreign Correspondents' Club, but we also had educational seminars and workshops, cocktail parties, pool parties, and even costume parties.

At one costume party Bunny wowed everyone by appearing as a sumo wrestler, although her chest was discreetly covered. And sometimes, instead of serious speeches, we had Japanese comic *rakugo* monologues and *manzai*-type dialogues in English. The Americans were clever, uninhibited, and knew how to enjoy themselves, and most of us Japanese members learned to relax and laugh and play with them. Both Americans and Japanese benefited from the association. It was a beautiful experience to see young adults from different cultures having fun communicating with each other.

One day Bunny asked me to head FCC's special projects committee. I wasn't sure about what such a committee would do and asked for guidance.

"Well," she said, "FCC was born in Tokyo and most of its members are Americans. Wouldn't it be nice if FCC could contribute something to the local community?"

I was amazed. Today, Japanese corporations operating in the United States are proud to talk about corporate philanthropy, most of it involving monetary gifts. But at that time, members of a small group of young and not particularly affluent Americans were thinking about contributing something to the foreign society in which they found themselves.

"Great idea," I said. "But don't you think one of the Americans ought to head the committee?"

"No," she said. "It's important that the committee chairman be a local person very familiar with his society, who is aware of its needs and knows how we can help. But really, the nationality of the chairman doesn't matter. It's understanding that's important."

I could not turn her down. This was the same kind of message I had heard in Los Angeles in my activities with the Lions Club. What thoughtful, perceptive people Americans are, I thought.

At the time "internationalization" was a buzzword in Japanese business circles. Speakers on this subject were in high demand, especially in areas outside major centers like Tokyo and Osaka. JETRO, which had about thirty offices around the country, often was asked by local organizations to provide programs on internationalization. But to be effective the speakers had to make their presentations in Japanese and there weren't enough Japanese knowledgeable on the subject to meet the need. Well, FCC had members who could speak in Japanese. One of my committee's first projects was a speaker's bureau.

On one occasion I accompanied Ron McFaren, who worked for Isuzu Motor Co., to the city of Himeji to talk to a group of young men studying management at the Kansai Institute for Small Business Management and Technology. Some of them had recently inherited a family business from their fathers. The class was preparing to tour the United States as part of their education, and Ron told them what they could expect. After his lecture, there was a question-and-answer session, and one of the students asked me what he should talk about when he met an American business manager.

"I think it would be useful," I said, "if you told him what you do. Tell him about the biggest problem in your company, and explain how you plan to solve it. Then you can ask about his problems and how he has solved them. You will find Americans interested in learning about your problems and rewards, and they will be willing to tell you about their experiences. If you open up, he will open up and it will be a rewarding session for both of you. Learning about what people are doing and have done is better than simply discussing opinions about U.S.-Japanese relations."

Ron nodded approval. Because he could converse with the students in fluent Japanese he enjoyed a credibility that enhanced the value of the FCC program.

Early on, I found that the presence of even one or two white faces in FCC's forays outside of Tokyo boosted the sense of "internationalization" that our hosts craved. This led to a major expedition to the city of Kanazawa, in Ishikawa Prefecture on the Japan Sea side of Honshu, the main island, where the JETRO office wanted to sponsor a seminar.

A number of FCC members wanted to visit Japan off the beaten track, but in this case our largest problems were scheduling and budgeting because each member would be paying his or her own expenses. And because most of our members worked during the week, they could get away only on weekends. We could leave Tokyo for Kanazawa by train on a Friday night and return on Sunday night, but that would be an exhausting journey with minimal time in Kanazawa. Air travel would be more practical. The problem was that round-trip airfare would be about ¥20,000, which we figured was about equal to the total of what each member could afford to spend on such a voluntary mission. Ultimately the

Ishikawa prefectural government offered to meet all our expenses in Kanazawa if we could get there on our own.

The Hokuriku Economic Federation, made up of the governments of the adjoining Ishikawa, Toyama, and Fukui Prefectures; the regional power company and other private interests, was planning a mission to the United States to attract investments. What they sought from FCC was help in preparing for the mission: polishing their English-language speeches, reviewing slide shows, editing the texts of brochures, and the like.

Nineteen members of FCC, thirteen Americans and six Japanese, made the trip. It was a very useful experience for most of the Americans, who had never been outside of the major cities. On the first night we were housed at a Buddhist temple—a frugal and not uncommon practice—where we slept on the floor and ate traditional foods. And just before we left at the end of our mission, we were entertained at a reception, not at a fancy hotel as was customary, but a potluck dinner in a community hall.

Our group was divided into three teams: One team spent much of its time with government officials. The second visited with representatives of the economic federation. And the third team spent time at local colleges and high schools meeting with English-language students who had had little opportunity to speak with native English-speakers.

Between the formal meetings there were many informal discussions between the visitors and local citizens on such subjects as business practices and etiquette, education, marriage and family, and women in the workplace.

Regardless of whether our efforts resulted in more American business coming into the Hokuriku area, FCC's trip was an extremely effective venture into international understanding at the grassroots level.

Later on, FCC extended its reach with a video titled *Making It in Japan: Can It Be Done?* It was a volunteer project that took nine months to complete, but we had professional direction. Jane Condon, an American magazine writer who later wrote a well-received book about Japanese women titled *A Half Step Behind,* gave much of her time to the project. Another participant was Machiko Minegishi, producer/director at an English-language television channel in Tokyo. I will have more to say about her later.

The cost of the video project was estimated at ¥2 million, a huge sum for a volunteer group, but we decided to take it on without knowing where a single yen was coming from. When I went to talk about the project with Takashi Kobayashi, vice president of JCTV television station, he showed enough faith to offer use of their production staff and facilities without charge in exchange for broadcasting rights. The American 3M company donated the tape. And Dick Yamashita, president of Marcom International, with whom I had worked on the American Chamber of Commerce Trade Study Group project, offered to cover cash expenditures.

Figuring that the content of the video was more important than action or visual beauty in helping newly arrived Americans to better understand Japan, we settled on the format of interviews with four Americans living in

Tokyo: a male executive of a large U.S. corporation, a woman of Japanese descent employed as manager of an American cosmetics company, a male fluent in Japanese and married to a Japanese who was a manager at a Japanese securities company, and a female copywriter from Hawaii working for a small public relations firm. All related their experience of living and working in Japan. In addition, Donald Richie, film critic, writer, and longtime Japan specialist, made some general remarks.

The video may have seemed dull to the casual viewer, but it was praised for providing useful information about living in Japan, both the good and the bad. It received complimentary press reviews when it was aired. Bernard Buck, a visiting news director from a New York TV station, saw one of the reviews and asked for a copy of the video. I was told it was aired three times in New York City.

Eventually, other responsibilities made it necessary for me to leave FCC, but I never regretted the time I spent with the organization. Most of the members were young, enthusiastic, eager to learn about Japan, and happy to share knowledge about their native America with the Japanese. The last I heard, Bunny Cramer, who brought me into FCC, is now living in Boston. The second and third presidents, George Faas and Peggy Aizawa, are in Irvine, California.

As the number of Americans working in Japan increased, other similar organizations have been founded. Among them are the Foreign Executive Women and the Kaisha Society.

All such organizations perform a useful service in helping foreigners adjust to life and work in Japan, and in helping the Japanese to understand everyday Americans. I am pleased to see so many young foreigners coming to Japan to live and work, and that they have places now to share both their concerns and aspirations among themselves and with the Japanese.

CHAPTER 13

The Tide Turns

FOR TWO DECADES AFTER BEING CRUSHED in World War II, Japan was regarded by much of the world as an impoverished nation desperately exporting—mostly cheap and shoddy stuff—to rebuild its economy. The Commonwealth of Puerto Rico was the first to realize times were changing—that Japan soon would be ready to export capital in addition to its products—and did something about it.

Puerto Rico sent an official mission to Japan in 1965 to solicit direct investment, to bring in Japanese money to build job-producing factories and businesses. Even then the idea of Japan investing abroad seemed far-fetched. In 1965, for the first time Japan enjoyed a trade surplus with the United States, a modest $113 million. No one could foresee the day when that surplus would exceed $50 billion, and a decade or more was to pass before other nations followed Puerto Rico's lead.

I have no way of knowing how Puerto Rico's mission was greeted in Japan. I was stationed in New York City at the time, working to fuel my country's domestic economic growth by promoting markets for its manufactured goods. The Japanese must have been startled to learn someone wanted their investments as well. There is no record of Puerto Rico's 1965 efforts in the authoritative *History of JETRO's Three Decades*.

But perhaps in some way I had been partly responsible for their decision to woo Japanese investments. Early in 1965, some months before Puerto Rico's mission to Japan, JETRO's deputy director in New York, Sueaki Oda, and I visited Puerto Rico at the invitation of Geoffrey U. Uyehara, the New York representative of the commonwealth's Economic Development Administration. It was a delightful trip with bright sunshine and balmy temperatures, in contrast to New York's grimy winter. Uyehara escorted us on visits to the plants of General Electric Instruments Corp., Caribe Circuit Breaker, Union Carbide, and other American corporations. At every stop the American manager would tell us how the skilled and modestly paid local labor made it effective and economical to manufacture in Puerto Rico. At the Economic Development Administration we were briefed about foreign trade zones and tax incentives for foreign businesses.

Puerto Rico's mission to Tokyo soon followed. What the visitors may not have known is that foreign currency was still restricted in Japan, and it was difficult to get permission even for overseas travel. And since investments abroad were strictly controlled, nothing came of Puerto Rico's mission until years later. Today there is much Japanese business activity in Puerto Rico.

After Puerto Rico's pioneering mission, it took another half dozen years—during which Japan's exports boomed, the trade surplus grew, the economy improved vastly, and currency restrictions were eased—for the United States to follow Puerto Rico's lead. American governors, mayors, and corporation chiefs heading trade and investment missions began to arrive in Japan in a steady stream. And almost all of them asked JETRO to arrange seminars at which they could make a sales pitch.

Simultaneously, many states set up representative offices in Tokyo. Their primary goal was to attract Japanese investment, and the competition between states was vigorous. By the early 1980s, more than thirty U.S. states had opened offices in prestigious sections of downtown Tokyo where the rent was exorbitant. Most of them consisted of a director from the state, who often knew little about Japan, a Japanese assistant director, and a bilingual secretary. Only a few states hired a Japanese director. In time the representatives formed the American States Offices Association, which would meet regularly at the U.S. Embassy to discuss their problems. My office was high on their list of information sources, and I, as head of the Overseas Public Relations Department, became friendly with many of them.

One of our functions was to respond to American requests for help in organizing investment seminars. Typically the procedure would start with a call from a state's representative informing us that his governor was coming next month with a delegation of very important politicians and businessmen. Could we set up a seminar in JETRO's meeting room where they could tell potential investors about the advantages their area offered for building a factory or distribution center?

Reserving the meeting room was the easiest part. In addition we had to get out the publicity, hire interpreters, make up an invitation list, arrange for press coverage, and see that a high JETRO official would be present to honor the Americans. In effect JETRO, free of charge, provided services that a consultant might undertake for a handsome fee. More precisely, since JETRO is a government-sponsored organization, Japanese taxpayers were paying for a program to lure investments abroad.

The more successful these seminars were, the busier my staff and I became. But before long, each seminar was no more than a mind-dulling copy of the previous one, the chief difference being the name of the state or city sponsoring it. Every state and city was selling essentially the same product—inexpensive land, a reliable and intelligent labor force, tax incentives, friendly people—and it wasn't easy to make a different sales pitch. Getting representatives of Japanese companies to attend became a growing problem because they weren't hearing what they wanted to know.

A partial list of trade missions in my 1978 calendar shows that in January, we arranged major seminars for the state of Washington, Belgium, and Great Britain; in February, Florida; in March, Pennsylvania; in May, Tennessee and Connecticut; in June, Quebec province; and in July, Indiana and Texas. That gives you an idea of the workload. April isn't listed because I was in Europe for a conference of JETRO overseas directors, but my office had to take care of the usual load.

One day in the spring of 1978, the economic development director of an American midwestern city telephoned to ask us to organize a seminar the following month. I explained that attendance at seminars had been very poor and suggested he might be more successful if his mission visited corporations, which we could target for him. But he insisted on a seminar, saying he would be satisfied if just two or three people with serious intentions showed up. Well, I told myself, if that's all he wants, we'll go ahead and schedule his group along with three others coming the same month.

We sent out invitations and promoted the seminar just as we would always do, and I was distressed that there were only two acceptances. I couldn't bear the thought of presenting our overseas visitors with a nearly empty meeting room, so I cajoled several young JETRO employees to attend and present the appearance of being possible investors. "You will learn some important things," I told them, even though their function was only to fill chairs.

Why was JETRO, representing the Japanese government, making such efforts to help America acquire investments from Japan? Because it had grown obvious that Japan's trade surplus with the United States would not be reduced simply by promoting U.S. exports to Japan. Some of our dollars, acquired in sales of Japanese products to Americans, ought to be sent back in the form of investments that would perform double duty by creating jobs for the Americans.

The American Chamber of Commerce in Japan (ACCJ) was as concerned as I was about the fall in seminar attendance and agreed that the teams from the U.S. simply were not providing the kind of information that potential investors wanted. ACCJ's investments committee, headed by Rodney Quainton from the First National City Bank of Chicago, and I decided our two organizations could be of service to both Japanese and Americans and could save everyone a lot of money by organizing seminars locally. Americans already in Japan, familiar with both countries, would be the speakers. We scheduled six sessions over a period of seven months, and to meet our costs and place a value on these seminars we set a modest registration fee.

We were on the right track. More than 700 Japanese businessmen participated. We covered such subjects as the American tax system, labor-management relations, the judicial system, demographic patterns, the distribution system, the relationship between states and the federal government, and the like. The session on U.S. labor and management drew such a large attendance that we had to move it from JETRO's largest seminar room to the U.S. Embassy's auditorium.

Up to that time, JETRO's efforts had been regarded by many Americans in business or government largely as window dressing to cover up Japan's growing trade surplus. Trade friction and deteriorating U.S.-Japanese relations had become a regular media topic. But the success of the joint

ACCJ and JETRO sessions opened a few eyes. And recognizing the demand in Japan for information about investing in America, we began to think about reverse missions: taking Japanese to the United States to explore at first hand opportunities for investment.

But now we ran into problems with ACCJ. They wanted to send invitations only to companies that had attended our seminars. I wanted to invite a much greater number, including many mid-sized firms. The larger companies either have overseas offices already or know where to get the information they need, I argued. It is the smaller, innovative companies without extensive resources that need our help. The people who came to our seminars usually were not top officials in position to affect decisions, and it is unlikely that invitations sent to them would get past their desks, I warned.

I also pointed out that small to midsized companies depend heavily on guidance from their banks in making business decisions. Banks certainly should be part of our delegation. Eventually we agreed on a mailing list and other details, and followed up the invitations with personal calls in an effort to recruit at least thirty organizations that would be willing to let a representative go abroad for a month. This experience of working very closely with hard-headed American businessmen strengthened my conviction that though they had strong ideas and were not reluctant to push them, they could see other points of view and were willing to modify their positions if they were convinced of the merits.

Ultimately we received many more applicants than we could accommodate because of logistical problems. Owing to the limitations of hotel accommodations and airline seats, we set a quota of forty-five business representatives plus eight staff. All but one of the businessmen were manufacturers interested in setting up operations in the States. This pleased ACCJ. Minoru Masuda, who later was to serve as JETRO chairman, headed the delegation. There were three of us from JETRO. Hiromi Ushijima represented the U.S. Embassy, and Thomas Nevins the American Chamber.

To accommodate as much as possible the varied interests of the individual members, the United States was divided into five areas based on five JETRO offices that were used as bases of operations. For example, when the entire delegation went to Chicago, the members were given a choice of taking off to visit St. Louis, Missouri; Battle Creek, Michigan; Joliet-Kankakie, Illinois;. Milwaukee, Wisconsin; Cincinnati, Ohio; or Kansas City, Missouri. The local governments in each of these places provided transportation from Chicago and back, and in one state the governor's plane was put at our disposal.

Other tours were scheduled out of New York City, Atlanta, Houston, and Los Angeles. Everywhere, the Japanese visitors were welcomed warmly. The project, originally called the Investment Mission, was renamed the Investment Development Mission to avoid the impression that the visitors were actually ready to invest. All together the mission visited seventeen states in sixteen days, touring twelve industrial parks and interviewing the Japanese managers of twenty-four companies already operating in the U.S. Among their products were TV sets, fire alarms, beauty salon equipment, telephone components, auto parts, toys, and even chewing gum and instant noodles.

The Japanese felt welcomed wherever they went. In one city the mayor met them in an official welcome at which a band played the national anthem of both nations.

Perhaps the most valuable part of the project was the opportunity to talk with the Japanese managers of Japanese plants operating in the United States. The visitors didn't need interpreters to ask about local successes and problems, or to learn about the reason for their move to the States, how they were able to deal with American workers, the problems they had with regulations, their reception in the community, and many other matters that were rarely covered in seminars in Tokyo.

This was the first of many successful JETRO tours, but in time, Japanese companies no longer required our assistance. One recent survey shows that at the end of March, 2000, 2126 Japanese companies were operating plants in the United States.

Chapter 14

The Rising Surplus

Despite all our efforts, Japan's trade surplus with the United States, and the world for that matter, continued to grow. Japan experienced its first postwar surplus in 1965 when imports were $8.2 billion, compared to exports of $8.5 billion—a net of $300 million in Japan's favor. Of that amount, a $113 million surplus was with the United States.

In 1970, five years later, the balance in Japan's favor was $380 million, and a year after that it soared to $2.5 billion. The trend continued to $3.0 billion in 1972, $3.9 billion in 1976, $7.3 billion in 1977, and $10.1 billion in 1978. The surplus dropped to $6 billion in 1979, but by 1990, Japan's trade surplus with the U.S. exceeded $38 billion and its world surplus was $52 billion.

Japanese newspapers featured stories almost daily that American concern about the imbalance was growing into anger that the nation that had crushed Japan in war—and helped it to get back on its feet—was now being defeated economically. In Congress there were demands for drastic action to curb imports from Japan.

By this time JETRO was spending more time and effort promoting imports rather than exports, but some elements of the public opposed the change of course. Remembering the difficult years immediately after the war and the effort and sacrifice it took to rebuild the economy, people asked questions. Many asked whether it was appropriate for the government to use taxpayer money to help foreign companies compete in Japan against domestic producers that only lately had become prosperous. Shouldn't it be the responsibility of competitor nations to spend their own money to promote sales in the Japanese market? Shouldn't trade be something for private industry to deal with? Doesn't America, Japan's longtime "big brother," feel ashamed about complaining about Japan's success?

After spending most of my career "selling" Japan, I found myself deeply involved in selling America to the Japanese. As early as 1972 the Japan U.S. Economic Council had sent twenty-six trade specialists on a tour of six American cities: Los Angeles, Kansas City, Dallas, Atlanta, New York, and Minneapolis. It was called the Mission to Promote U.S. Exports to Japan, reflecting Japan's belief that the solution to trade problems was not to restrict Japanese sales in the United States, but rather to balance trade by increasing American sales in Japan. And I must state that Japan was making strenuous efforts to help Americans promote their products.

The following year, 1973, the Chicago Chamber of Commerce and Industry sponsored an Export to Japan fair at the Navy Pier where, so many years earlier, Ippei Takeda and I had manned a Japan booth and displayed products like cameras. This time more than 650 Japanese merchandisers showed up to search for products they could sell back home. At about this time, three large Japanese trading companies were handling 94 percent of American exports to Japan and it was a difficult task to interest small and midsized American companies in entering the Japanese market directly.

I am firmly of the belief that the marketplace—not politics—should resolve trade problems, but where large sums of money and economic well-being are at stake, it is inevitable that governments become involved. In September 1977, shortly after I had returned to Tokyo following my three-year assignment in Los Angeles, a conference was held between Juanita Kreps, the U.S. Secretary of Commerce, and Tatsuo Tanaka, minister of International Trade and Industry. As a result, another high-level promotion mission went to the United States in March 1978. It was headed by Yoshizo Ikeda, president of the powerful Mitsui and Co., and included ninety-two members representing various consumer segments. Over a two-week period they visited seventeen cities.

Their mission was to buy American products; to meet with government, business, labor, and media leaders; to confer with representatives of Japanese trading companies in the U.S.; and to encourage American businessmen to participate in export seminars being held by JETRO representatives in various parts of the country. Members of the mission also purchased about $50 million worth of American products, including what they felt obliged to buy as well as items they needed.

In return, a 138-member American mission came to Japan six months later. It was headed by Secretary Kreps and Mark Shepherd, chairman of Texas Instruments, who at the time was considered a leading Japan-basher. This made some Japanese nervous but I was pleased to have an opportunity to show him firsthand what Japan was like. JETRO established a thirty-seven-member task force, including me, to prepare for their arrival.

JETRO Chairman Hisashi Murata presents U.S. Commerce Secretary Anita Kreps a symbolic key to the Japanese Market. October 5, 1978.

JETRO was accustomed to providing VIP treatment for important foreign visitors, but this was not an ordinary VIP visit. The day before Secretary Kreps was to arrive, all the furniture in Chairman Murata's office was hauled out and a new sofa, desks, and chairs—all rented—were brought in. I wondered whether it wouldn't have been better tactics to retain the worn and threadbare furniture to give the impression that Japan was not rolling in wealth. But upgrading the furnishings wasn't the only evidence of nervousness. Later I learned that there had been intense discussions about whether the visitors should be served coffee, Japanese green tea, or orange juice. As I recall, the problem was solved by offering all three.

What would happen in an American trade organization preparing for the visit of a Japanese dignitary? Nobody asked me, but I could have told anyone that in all probability the staff would brief the boss on the background of the Japanese visitors, current issues, and matters that likely would be brought up, and that would be all the preparation necessary for candid and cordial conversation.

My role on this occasion was to draft a speech for one of the senior officials to greet the Americans at a meeting to begin at 8 A.M. the day following their arrival. A typical Japanese speech would begin something like this: "I am Mr. So-and-So, and I am going to make a short speech."

But I knew the Americans had spent a dozen hours in an airplane, were suffering from jet lag, and probably had not slept well. I figured they could use a little levity.

The speech I wrote started,"Good morning, and welcome to Japan. I congratulate you on overcoming Japanese's toughest non-tariff trade barrier—getting from Narita Airport to downtown Tokyo on our terribly crowded highways."

The Japanese at the meeting looked at each other nervously, but the Americans laughed in appreciation and the ice was broken.

JETRO was responsible for setting up appointments, escorting the Americans wherever they wished to go, and providing all manner of background information. We felt amply repaid when Mark Shepherd declared in one of his speeches: "We came to Japan to sell American goods, but there is one thing we wouldn't mind taking back with us. That is JETRO. Without JETRO's help we would not be nearly as successful as we were."

It was difficult for Americans to understand that JETRO, a government agency, was so dedicated to promoting American exports to Japan. But once someone like Mark Shepherd, the chairman of a giant corporation anxious to sell to Japan, acknowledged our efforts, it was most encouraging.

We followed up the Kreps mission with another project designed to introduce American consumer goods to ordinary citizens in remote areas of Japan. The idea was to lease an ocean liner, stock it with a wide variety of American products, and send it out to as many port cities as possible, like a traveling department store, with Japanese visitors able to buy items directly off the shelves. My

American counterparts were somewhat skeptical at first, but to their credit they were willing to give it a try.

We took care of the logistics and the American side took care of assembling some 800,000 pieces of merchandise from 145 different companies: textiles, home appliances, sporting goods like golf clubs and skis, and food items. The Americans also gave the project a name: Boatique America, a combination of "boat" and "boutique." The ship, called the *Shin Sakura Maru,* called at thirteen ports between October 12 and November 9, 1979. Ironically, this same ship had been used earlier as a floating showcase to promote Japanese products. Now it was being converted to promote American goods.

Many organizations—MITI, the Japan Industrial Cruise Exhibition Association, the Chamber of Commerce of Japan, the Manufactured Imports Promotion Organization, and prefectural and city organizations—got into the act. But most of the planning and execution of those plans were the work of an eighty-member JETRO task force. Not least of the duties of its members was visiting the various ports of call and asking for the cooperation of everyone concerned.

The tour was launched with a gala ceremony in Tokyo attended by Ambassador Mike Mansfield and gaggles of Japanese dignitaries. The next day, when the exhibit was opened to the public, people had been waiting in line for three hours before they were permitted aboard at 10 A.M.

In the fifty-one days the exhibit was open, more than 476,000 visitors were recorded, with purchases of ¥954 million. The most popular item was American beef, then under a strict import quota. Each day's supply sold out quickly. The next five most popular items were women's wear, kitchen utensils, towels, sporting goods, and children's clothing. (Since that time, imports of American beef have been greatly liberalized and now are available in Japanese supermarkets at prices comparable to those in the United States.)

I was not involved in the merchandising aspects of the Boatique America project, but from my point of view it was a rousing success, proving that if the products Japanese want are properly promoted and made available, they will buy regardless of origin. When I reported my views at a meeting of the American Chamber of Commerce in Japan, a member of the U.S. Embassy staff rose to contradict me. From the American perspective, he said, the project was a one-shot and ineffective in the long run, and product-specific trade shows were preferable.

But Robert F. Connelly, who had been in business in Japan for many years, praised the Boatique America project. He said he had visited all thirteen ports of call and used the opportunity to find many new clients. "If Americans want to succeed here," he said, "they can't just go home in a week or two. They have to work at it."

In a way, both the diplomat and my friend Connelly were right. When we have to take action mainly for political reasons, an attention-getting project such as Boatique America can be very helpful. But in striving for a general increase in exports, a less flamboyant approach like product-specific trade shows may be the way to go, despite the record of ineffectiveness. What impressed me more than what was said at the meeting was the refreshing sight of a small-businessman standing up in public and contradicting a government official without fear of reprisal. Of course I knew that in the States, no love was lost between government and business, but I was pleased and not a little surprised that it was happening in Japan even though no Japanese were involved.

Chapter 15

The Guy in Charge

In any large organization it seems inevitable that someone who is reasonably successful in some responsibility is promoted to take on other responsibilities whether he or she likes it or not. This is particularly true in Japanese organizations, where executives are considered generalists rather than specialists and are moved from one post to another.

In 1983, after having spent most of my twenty-six years at JETRO in one aspect of public relations or another, I was named director of the General Affairs Department. This responsibility included supervision of public relations functions plus general operations, personnel matters, wages, and benefits.

Two years later, in June 1985, I was named one of six executive directors of JETRO. It was a prestigious position. Among the perquisites were a car and driver, which are considered very important in Japan. I became responsible for the activities and budgeting of JETRO offices in fifty-seven nations. I also had supervision over the Trade Fair Department, which arranged trade fairs both overseas and in Japan because of the emphasis on imports. Additionally, I had supervision over opening new JETRO offices, which was not easy because of the "scrap and build policy"—for budgetary purposes an office had to be closed before a new one was opened. The drawback to all this was that the director's primary function was not to innovate, but to review and approve proposals from below. In fact, etiquette demanded that an executive director not become involved in work and planning sessions unless invited. I missed the action and give-and-take that occurred at the working level.

Thus I was pleased with a revolutionary personnel policy, which I had largely instigated, that enabled JETRO to take a more active role in helping other countries—in this case the United States—to build business in Japan. It started before my elevation to executive director when I received a telex message from Gary Miller, director of the international division at the state of Connecticut's Department of Commerce. He said the president of a Connecticut firm called Omega Engineering, a woman named Betty Holander, would be joining a trade promotion mission that President Reagan would be sending to Japan, and asked me to talk with her.

I met Mrs. Holander and her husband, Milton, in January 1984 at a reception at the Okura Hotel. She said she was working to establish a Connecticut state office in Japan and asked for my opinion about what would be the most important factor in ensuring its success once it was opened.

"That's an easy one," I told her. "You will have a difficult time succeeding unless you have the right person running the office."

Some months later I received word from a delighted Mrs. Holander that the Connecticut state legislature had approved a trade promotion office in Japan. Soon, she, Gary Miller, and John Carson, director of Connecticut's Economic Development Bureau, came to Tokyo to help set up the office.

In one of our discussions Carson astonished me by asking whether he could borrow someone temporarily from JETRO to head his state's office.

"Well," I stammered, "that's never been done before. I'll have to think about it."

As the discussion continued, we agreed that the person on loan would have to be very competent, have a pleasant personality, and have a good command of English and a working knowledge of Americans and the American way of doing business. JETRO would not want to lose the services of such a person, even temporarily, but on the other hand he would continue to be promoting JETRO's primary objective, which was to increase imports. By the time I agreed to the proposal, I had a specific person in mind.

He was Fujiya Yamagata, a graduate of Mankato State University in Minnesota, who had been stationed by JETRO in Los Angeles and Singapore. He was fluent in English, didn't hesitate to try new ideas, and had a good personality. Yamagata welcomed the idea of working for Connecticut on a temporary basis. On October 1, 1985, shortly after I was named an executive director, the Connecticut office was opened with Yamagata in charge. Some time later a similar request came from the state of Michigan and a JETRO employee named Joji Hara, who had been in our Chicago office, took the assignment.

The loan of personnel worked out very well and I was pleased with the opportunity of JETRO employees to get the experience of working in an American office. But I ran into unexpected opposition from some members of the American State Offices Association (ASOA), made up of Americans working in Japan as state representatives.

Several felt that state offices manned by a JETRO employee would have an unfair advantage in the Japanese market. Others feared that in time they might be replaced by a JETRO staff person. I explained that Yamagata and Hara were on temporary loan while the state offices were becoming established and had no connection with JETRO during the period of detached employment, that they were being paid by their American employers, and that JETRO would continue to support all states equally. The Americans were satisfied only when JETRO agreed to put all this in writing.

This arrangement proved to be so effective that ten years later, JETRO had expanded the program to include recruiting as many as thirty-five successful people from Japanese firms and loaning them to fourteen countries to help them develop exports to Japan. They were called senior trade advisers. They were given leave by their companies, and their salaries and expenses were paid by JETRO. Their assignment was to scour their areas for local products that might have a market in Japan and help with their export. In the U.S., senior trade advisers were allocated to twenty-two states. The states provided office space and secretarial help and the trade advisers worked closely with their local counterparts.

Such efforts were quite in contrast to official American efforts to reduce Japan's trade surplus, which by 1984 had risen to an alarming $33 billion. In March of that year, JETRO proposed a "Made in USA Fair" in Nagoya, Japan's third largest city, to be sponsored jointly by JETRO and the U.S. Department of Commerce. There have been many complaints about the Japanese bureaucracy, but I must say that in this case the Department of Commerce was no better. The first requirement in seeking cosponsorship for the event was to submit an application to the department. It was returned with a request for more information. Time and again our revised proposals were returned with requests for modifications or more details. Eventually the fair was held, and 190 of the 250 participating American companies reported they were very satisfied with the results. JETRO had assigned seventy-five members of the staff fulltime to the project benefiting American companies, and covered all local expenses.

Such expenses were not insignificant. Expert interpreters for meetings between potential Japanese buyers and American supplies can cost from $200 to $400 an hour. Carpenters needed to put up booths, and displays were in the same price range. And all this was being underwritten by the Japanese taxpayer.

Despite these efforts, Japan's trade surplus with the United States had grown by 1985 to $39 billion, with no sign of slowing. To make the point that no import item was insignificant no matter how small, Prime Minister Yasuhiro Nakasone appeared on national television to display an American necktie he had purchased and urged every Japanese to go out and buy $100 worth of imported goods. The prime minister's necktie was simply an eye-catching symbol of what was possible.

In January 1985, the American and Japanese governments began what were called the Market Oriented Sector Selective (MOSS) talks to promote trade in telecommunications equipment, pharmaceuticals and medical items, electronics including supercomputers, and forestry products. Later, transportation equipment, including automobile parts, was brought into the talks. The U.S. contended that

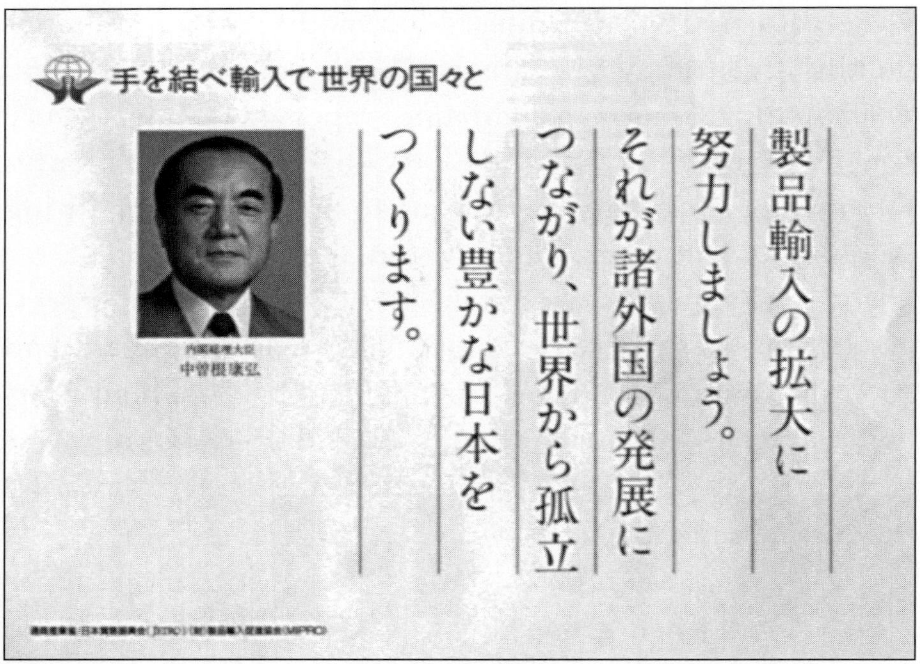

On April 9, 1985, Prime Minister Yasuhiro Nakasone took the unprecedented action of asking every Japanese person to buy $100 worth of imported goods. This flyer distributed in connection with his campaign, said: "Let's try to increase imports of foreign goods. That will enhance the development of other countries and build wealthy Japan without isolating from the international society."

extremely detailed import regulations prevented these products from entering the Japanese market and announced its intention of dismantling them one by one. Both governments acknowledged the importance of the MOSS meetings and within a year the U.S reported increased exports of these various products.

Meanwhile Japan, through JETRO, continued its efforts to promote American goods. As an executive director I became involved in U.S. product bazaars in Tokyo, which drew 410,000 attendees; in Yokoyama, with 320,000; and Kitakyushu in the south, 260,000. These were followed by a number of smaller bazaars where all manner of American-made products were made available to Japanese consumers. Although the United States received most of the attention, Europe was not forgotten. At a fair in Kobe early in 1986, a total of 140 European companies exhibited a wide variety of products, including textile manufacturing machinery.

Early on, I could see that these broad-based fairs were unwieldy and not as effective as they should be for the time and effort expended. This led to my decision to implement three policies:

1. Each sales promotion fair would focus on certain related products.
2. The products to be featured would be in an area where Japanese needs might rise in the future.
3. New trade shows would not be in industries and products featured in the recent past.

In keeping with this policy, an import fair in March 1987, featured American-made medical equipment and health industry supplies. Although Japan was quite advanced in the medical sciences, Japanese hospitals and care centers were wide open to innovations in the health service field. Moreover, as health care standards improved, the country was faced by an increasing population of the aged: the so-called silver market. Not exactly coincidentally, I proposed the health care fair at a time when the MOSS meetings were addressing medical equipment exports. Obviously such a fair would carry a strong message to Americans about the Japanese desire to increase imports from the U.S.

Broad cooperation was necessary to make this focused fair a success, particularly from the Ministry of Health and Welfare. I approached them with concern, remembering that I had been called an "American agent" by some bureaucrats on earlier occasions. I needn't have worried. My contact in the Health and Welfare Ministry was Hiroyuki Yanai, who was responsible for testing new medical equipment. He proved to be understanding and cooperative and met with a planning committee to offer suggestions.

But the medical fair would not be successful without strong American participation. Instead of waiting for the Americans to take the initiative, I persuaded several of the large Japanese trading companies to send medical equipment specialists to the U.S. to urge American companies to participate. JETRO offices in the U.S. made a special effort to get the word out to manufacturers. The fair opened in

March 1987 with a slogan coined by a friend, Warren Day: "Good Health to You from America."

It was only a four-day fair, but the attendance totaled 15,563 and ultimately a gratifying 12,412 business deals were consummated. In addition to the exhibits, JETRO offered seminars for American exhibitors explaining the Japanese way of doing business. We also made tours of Japanese medical facilities available for the American visitors, and scheduled seminars by eminent American medical scientists who had been specially invited to the fair.

The health fair was so successful that we held an expanded version two years later. Its name was changed to JETRO Health Care '89 and it included all of North America, Europe, and Oceania. The medical fairs are held every other year and by 1995, when 280 exhibitors from sixteen nations participated, there was a waiting list of companies wishing to participate.

The "theme" idea was expanded in 1988 to a fair on sports and leisure products. In view of Japan's expanding interest in sports such as golf and skiing, and the leisure to enjoy such activities as hiking, camping, boating, and fishing, the show was an immediate success.

CHAPTER 16

Restlessness

DESPITE MY GRATIFYING SUCCESSES as an executive director of JETRO, before long I began to feel a need for a greater sense of fulfillment. I would be reaching retirement age in a few years and the prospect of simply sitting around after that was not inviting. I felt a desire to do something more about an interest that had been growing from my first temporary assignment in America—to advance understanding between the two countries—and I wanted the freedom to do it.

But how should it be done? I did not know. Perhaps it would be necessary to part company with JETRO, which had been the channel for promoting my hopes for so many years. The death of my wife, Renko, in 1987 added to my restlessness.

Renko has been mentioned only in passing in this book so far. That does not mean she was not deeply involved in my career. She was supportive of my activities in the uncomplaining way of a Japanese wife, but she was much more. In her quiet way she shared my aspirations to promote understanding between the Japanese people and the rest of the world. I must tell you about her.

I did not marry until 1959, when I was thirty, which in those days was not particularly old for a professional man in Japan. Part of the delay was due to the fact that I was trying to establish myself professionally. As I approached thirty, my mother began to suffer serious asthmatic seizures. Since marriage by Japanese custom is a family affair rather than an individual one, I kept putting off thoughts of finding a wife and settling down because I feared the entire complicated process would create an additional strain on my mother's health.

After a reasonable period following my mother's death, one of my sisters—don't sisters always have the well-being of younger brothers in mind?—showed me a photograph of a petite young woman named Renko Saito. My sister said a friend of hers knew Renko and wondered whether I would like to meet her. In the Japan of that time it was unusual for a young man to find his own marriage partner. It was the custom for a go-between—usually a friend of the parents—to locate what seemed to be a suitable mate and to arrange a meeting. The meeting is called a *miai*, which of course means "meeting," and is usually held at a restaurant dinner at which each party quietly scrutinizes the other. Either principal can call the whole thing off, but if they like what they see, a more private courtship begins.

I liked what I saw of Renko. I learned that her father was an actor named Tatsuo Saito who had been in a few Hollywood films. His wife had died when Renko was a baby and she had no memory of her mother. Tatsuo Saito married twice after that. One of the brides was a German girl who raised Renko. After this woman died, Saito married a woman about Renko's age. All this was a bit titillating. I thought Renko was attractive and of strong moral character and decided I would like to marry her.

Before anything could be arranged, JETRO sent me to the Chicago trade fair. When I returned I found my crusty old father, Shinji, stubbornly opposed to my marriage. He wanted nothing to do with a daughter-in-law whose father was a flamboyant show-business character. It took an old family friend named Kenzo Asahara to persuade my father to withdraw his objections.

My father changed his mind about Renko completely when he got to know her. Renko had studied nursing at a Catholic school and was attentive to his needs. He came to like her so much that from time to time he asked her to be his official hostess at public functions. Renko was outgoing and, unlike many Japanese women of the time, at ease with the Americans she met. When we lived in Los Angeles she was a volunteer at the nursing home for elderly Japanese immigrants. She gave me two fine daughters, Naoko, born in 1962, and Masako, in 1963. Shortly after our return from the Los Angeles assignment, Renko was diagnosed with a liver ailment; she died in 1987 after we had been married 28 years.

Renko's loss created a void that I tried to fill with many professional activities. One of them was the Trade Study Group (TSG), a lively organization whose membership was made up of Japanese and foreigners who attended because of their individual interests and not as representatives of particular businesses. Their lively concern with international understanding rekindled my interest in doing something to promote better relations between Japan and other nations, particularly the United States.

One of those I noticed at the meetings was a woman named Machiko Minegishi, who was a director and producer for Japan Cable Television. I first had met her when she came to JETRO to interview me, and she was a lively participant in the TSG discussions. She was forthright in expressing her ideas and I found myself agreeing with many of her views on how Japan should change to become a greater part of the family of nations.

Sometimes after the meetings, I would invite her to a coffee shop, where we continued our discussions. I told her of my still vague idea of leaving JETRO to pursue my interest in promoting international understanding and she listened intently. Eventually I began to realize that although I was past the age for a romantic second marriage, I was lonely for a partner who would share my interests.

One day I told Machiko that I had just about made up my mind to resign from JETRO and move to the United States, and although I had some ideas, I wasn't sure exactly what I would do there. I said I needed a partner with whom I could start a new life together, and then I asked if she would marry me and become that partner.

Earlier, Machiko had told me she had not married because she had never met anyone she wanted to be tied to. Now she accepted my proposal without a moment's hesitation.

"But don't say anything to anybody," she said, smiling mischievously. "I must tell my sister first."

Machiko's sister was dubious. "Why do you want to give up your freedom?" she asked. "Why do you want to marry such an old man?"

Machiko replied that she was gaining a new freedom and added that I wasn't all that much older than she.

We were married on March 6, 1990. I was then sixty years old and Machiko was forty-seven. We saw no need for the traditional wedding ceremony. Our marriage was solemnized simply by going to the ward office to register for the record that we were husband and wife. Some days later, we held a joyous reception at the American Club. I have never regretted marrying Machiko. Although we were so different—she outgoing and enthusiastic and I reserved—we became a team working together on projects we both loved.

Shortly after the marriage I went to see Shiro Miyamoto, the president of JETRO, and told him I wished to resign.

"Why?" he asked in agitation. "This is a surprise. Oh, this is distressing. Nothing like this has happened before. Are you unhappy? Have you been offered another job? Are you having health problems? Look, don't be hasty. Let's think about this."

Apparently he realized he could not change my mind. A few days later, Shigeo Kawamoto, the director of general affairs, came to my office. Kawamoto's mission was to learn what JETRO could do to help me after I resigned.

I told him I wanted to start a nonprofit organization in the United States with the goal of helping Japanese and

Americans to better understand each other. The details weren't clear in my mind, I said, but I knew I had to be careful not to infringe on other organizations, like the Japanese Embassy and consulates and their cultural programs, or JETRO itself. I explained frankly that my means were limited, but I wanted to be independent and not rely on anyone for support.

"Where will you do this," he asked. "Los Angeles?"

"No, no," I said. "I have lived there. Los Angeles is too large and confusing for what I have in mind. Maybe I will go to Denver. I have visited Denver and I like it."

Kawamoto reminded me that I would need an office, a secretary, a telephone, and office equipment. Whatever I did, I would need books and money for subscriptions to newspapers, magazines, and scholarly journals. "JETRO could help you with these expenses, and perhaps in return you could help the JETRO office in Denver from time to time," he suggested.

Then he explained something I already knew: It was not uncommon for organizations like JETRO to provide support for executives who want to work after retirement. It was a reward, a gratuity for past service, and a way of ensuring that the retirees would be available for consultation if needed.

In the end, I accepted with the understanding that I would receive their support for no more than the customary five years while establishing an organization, to be called Inter-Pacific Institute for Communication (IPIC). I also made it clear that the arrangement could be terminated at any time by either party.

I resigned from JETRO on October 1, 1990, and three weeks later, Machiko and I flew to Denver, where we had a few friends but only a vague idea about what we would do or how we would do it. Our financial resources consisted of some modest savings, my retirement allowance, and fortunately the rent from our condominium apartments in Tokyo. Both were in desirable areas, mine near the Meiji Shrine and Machiko's near the French Embassy, and commanded rents that were handsome by U.S. standards. (In fact, we soon found it was far less expensive to live in Denver than in Japan.) We purchased an attractive ranch-style house on a spacious lot in a Denver suburb and adjusted to middle-class American life. Although we were only a few miles from downtown, Machiko was delighted that bird feeders attracted a wide variety of birds. Squirrels and even a pair of little red foxes were regular visitors to our wooded backyard.

Meanwhile, both of us were busy making friends, learning about America in general and Denver in particular, and talking to as many people as possible in the search for a way to be of service. For a time Machiko and I shared box lunches once a week with local people interested in Japan and discussed various suggestions for some kind of newsletter.

Out of these discussions was born the idea for an eight-page, letter-sized monthly newsletter to be called *Understanding Japan*. It would carry some timely news, but its main features were to be explanations of aspects of Japanese culture and practices that might be confusing to Americans.

Volume 1, Number 1, was published with high expectations in April 1992. It had taken a year and a half to get started. The publisher was Inter-Pacific Institute for Communication, with Shinsaku Sogo as president. Machiko was the editor.

The main feature in the first issue was a detailed report on the mandatory recycling laws Japan had been forced to adopt because it lacked both resources and dump sites. Other features in the issue were a discussion of problems Japan faced in adopting a five-day school week, the new child-rearing law designed to help working women, the practice of corporations spending huge amounts to entertain customers, and efforts to define death so that laws pertaining to organ transplants could be expedited.

We mailed out copies to anyone who was interested. The first issue carried a notice that *Understanding Japan* would be published ten times a year and the subscription price was $30 in the United States, $35 for Canada and Mexico, and $45 elsewhere.

Publication of *Understanding Japan* was not inexpensive, and I wondered how we would pay for the printing until subscriptions began to come in. An unexpected source came to our aid. Many years earlier, when Tokyo land prices were moderate, my father, Shinji Sogo, who had been prominent as a businessman and government official (he is credited with visualizing the famous Shinkansen bullet train system and directing its construction), had invested in a parcel of real estate and placed it in the name of two sons, Kazuhei and me. After my career was established at JETRO I sold my share to Kazuhei and bought the condominium near Meiji Shrine. Meanwhile, Tokyo real estate prices soared. Now

Kazuhei, who was a railroad administrator, had had to sell the property and realized a very handsome profit. Although I no longer held ownership in the property, Kazuhei insisted it was only right to share half of his good fortune with me. He said he wanted to support my project and sent me an impressively large check. I accepted it humbly and gratefully, and drew on this money to support IPIC.

Understanding Japan's second issue featured a comparison of the compensation patterns of American and Japanese workers, a report on *karoshi* (death from overwork), and leisure activities in Japan. Not all the items were serious. One was about the Japanese love of pets like dogs, and the problem of disposing of their wastes when they are taken out for a stroll.

In some of its features *Understanding Japan* tried to explain problems caused by cultural differences. One story reported that many Japanese take it as a challenge or even an accusation when an American asks why. It cited an instance in which a Japanese speaker froze in confusion when an American asked why about a point he did not understand well. The article pointed out that a question something like "Would someone explain the reason for..." would avoid confusion and offense.

Editing even an eight-page newsletter took a great deal of time because of the research involved in ascertaining the accuracy of everything we printed. Take, for instance, an inquiry we received from Dr. John E. Endicott, a reader from Georgia. He wrote: "I enjoyed the article on 'an-pan' as I especially enjoy eating it. However, I was surprised that...you mention that bread was introduced 'around 1874.'

Aren't you a couple of centuries off? 'Pan' is from the Portuguese for bread, and they were only a memory in 1874."

Good question. The Portuguese were the first Europeans to reach Japan, starting in 1543. The missionary St. Francis Xavier arrived in 1549 and stayed about two years. These visitors brought European culture along with Christianity, and it is likely that bread was among their cultural gifts. But less than a century later, the Japanese, fearing European encroachment on their territory and culture, expelled all foreigners except for a few Dutch traders who were allowed to set up a settlement on a tiny island in Nagasaki harbor. Dr. Endicott was right in saying the Portuguese were but a memory in Japan in 1874. Our reply was as follows:

> The first Japanese to make Western-style bread is said to be Taro-zaemon Egawa. In 1862 he made bread at Nirayama in Izu, mainly for combat rations. Yasubei Kimura, the founder of Kimuraya Bakery, was teaching at a vocational aid center at the request of the Meiji government. One of his colleagues, Umekichi, a man who came from Nagasaki, knew how to make bread. Yasubei Kimura hired him and began making bread in the second year of the Meiji period (1869) 123 years ago.
>
> Except for very limited consumption by foreigners living in the settlement in Tsukiji, Kimuraya Bakery's bread did not sell well at all. Yasubei had to come out with a new idea and decided to combine a classic Japanese favorite, sweet azuki bean paste, and bread, making "an-pan."

> Kaishu Katsu, who played a major role in the Meiji Restoration, was then a chamberlain for Emperor Meiji, and presented "an-pan to the Emperor. To indicate those "an-pan" going to the Emperor, Kimuraya placed pickled cherry blossoms at the center of the "an-pan.". Yasubei completed his creation in Meiji 7 (1874) and presented it to the Emperor, and then in Meiji 8 launched a huge sales campaign. He even hired a ding-dong band which was quite eye-catching in those days. This year, Japanese bread makers are celebrating the 130th anniversary of Western-style breadmaking in Japan.

Tracking down this information was not easy, but Machiko and I felt it was necessary to get the facts. We went to the best possible source, the Kimuraya Bakery, which was still in business in Tokyo, and the executive director, Mr. Ishii, kindly provided details from the firm's historical record.

On another occasion, *Understanding Japan* tried to explain *Sumimasen,* a word expressing apology but having other meanings as well. We wrote:

> ABC News' "World News Tonight" (Feb. 20, 1992) showed a Japanese newlywed couple bowing deeply at their wedding reception and also elevator girls bowing deeply at a Japanese department store. The reporter commented: "Every day, everywhere, everyone here says they are sorry." Obviously they mixed up apologies and greetings. The Japanese do bow for both occasions, and use the same word "Sumimasen" for not only apologizing, but also for greeting,

> calling for attention, knocking on doors, and even for saying "thank you." A Japanese sushi chef, just after he arrived in Los Angeles, kept shouting "I am sorry. I am sorry" in English every time he served sushi at the counter, a time when he would say "sumimasen" in Japanese. Now he says confidently, "Tuna, Table 10."

Fortunately for us in search of material to print, and unfortunately for American-Japanese accord, such examples of misunderstanding were numerous. At a time when the U.S. economy was having problems, Japanese prime minister Kiichi Miyazawa expressed *dojo* for the U.S. The word means "sympathy," and that is how it was translated. However, the word was meant to convey the idea that Japan should share America's problems and work to improve the situation together. Bill Clinton, then governor of Arkansas and a presidential candidate, seized on Miyazawa's remarks to make a political point: "We've fallen so far, so fast, that the Prime Minister of Japan actually said he felt 'sympathy' for America. When I'm your President, the world won't look down on us with pity. They'll look up to us with respect."

The confusion between yes and no, which often blocks understanding between Americans and Japanese, was the subject for another item. It is worth reprinting in full:

> "When Japanese talk, their conversation has a certain rhythm to it, with responses by each party in turn that cause the conversation to go smoothly. It is called "aizuchi" which literally means to hammer alternately by two or more

blacksmiths. In other words, Japanese often nod and say, "Ah, so, hai-hai," quite frequently during their conversation which makes the speaker feel comfortable to know that the other person is listening. It does not have to be a sign of agreement. The Japanese do not use eye-contact, as Americans may, for that purpose. In fact, quite the opposite.

"Even at big business meetings Japanese executives may close their eyes. This is a sign either that he is listing to you very carefully (or that he is having an afternoon nap).

"When a Japanese is talking with an American on the phone, sometimes he or she feels uneasy, particularly when he is saying something very important and complicated, and does not hear verbal responses from the other end. The Japanese may say, "Hello, are you listening?" having become a little suspicious that the other was not, and the American may say, "Yes, of course. I am listening to you very carefully."

To make the situation even more confusing, the Japanese word *hai* is often translated incorrectly as "Yes, I agree." When an American businessman in Tokyo recently concluded a presentation about his products to a group of Japanese, he was quite confident that he had made the deal. However, the answer was negative. He became upset and said, "Why is it suddenly 'no'?

"All the way through my presentation you had been nodding and saying 'yes, yes.'" The reply, "Oh, yes, we were listening to you very carefully."

Understanding Japan's audience never grew large, but it was widely dispersed and appreciative. Eventually we had subscribers in every state, Canada, Japan, England, Australia, and a few other places.

Machiko and I also conducted symposia on Japan. We responded to many requests from primary and secondary schools in the Denver area, and several times we traveled to distant college campuses to give seminars having more to do with Japanese cultural practices than with politics or economics.

We also ventured into the book-publishing business. The first volume was one we could produce fairly quickly and felt was needed for a better understanding of Japan. The subject was the remarkably innovative and useful Japanese bullet train, the Shinkansen which, admittedly, Americans had heard much about. But they knew almost nothing about the man responsible for putting the project together and the struggles he had faced, and I felt the story should be told. It was incidental, I think, that this man was Shinji Sogo, who also happened to be my father. Familial pride was not involved in picking the subject; I felt it was simply a worthy story that Americans ought to know.

The major problem in writing such a book for an American audience was that the subject was no longer living and all the resource material was in Japanese. Machiko solved it by translating more than 500 pages of research into English. This was used, along with some personal research, by Bill Hosokawa, a former Denver newspaperman and author who has a working knowledge of Japanese. The book was titled *Old Man Thunder, Father of the Bullet Train,* and to avoid the long delay and uncertainty of using a commercial book publisher, I published it through an arm of IPIC called Sogo Way and distributed it widely to libraries.

Meanwhile, I had two other book projects under way. One was to be the recollections of Americans who were in Japan immediately after the war's end when the Japanese government and society were in chaos. I wanted to record their observations and feelings and to recognize their contributions to the reconstruction of the country. The other project is the present volume.

Chapter 17

The Bolt from the Blue

Sunday, January 18, 1998, was an unusually mild day. Machiko and I spent the morning on our normal Sunday chores. In mid-afternoon she worked awhile cleaning out the flower beds and then suggested we go for a walk. Not far from our home is the Highline Canal, a ditch carrying irrigation water in summer. In winter it is dry. A pleasant, wooded hiking trail follows its course, and area residents enjoy strolling over it during all seasons of the year. We walked a mile or two, relishing the fresh air and the sound of a few year-round birds. As dusk approached, Machiko suggested we go back to the house and drive to Alfalfa's, a supermarket featuring organic foods, where we could have soup and a sandwich at the snack bar before getting the groceries.

I remember that she picked up a tuna sandwich. Then it happened. Machiko dropped to the floor in a heap without a sound. I rushed to her side, calling her name. There was no response. Other shoppers crowded around us, trying to be helpful. Someone telephoned 911 for emergency medical help.

Machiko lay still, her eyes closed, totally unconscious. After what seemed to be an interminable time, an ambulance arrived, sirens screaming.

A medical technician tried to revive her, but there was no response. He filled a syringe with some kind of fluid and started to inject it into her arm.

The instant the needle pierced her skin, Machiko jerked, opened her eyes and cried "*Itai, itai,*" the Japanese words for "It hurts, it hurts." Then she looked at me and seemed to be completely normal.

The ambulance took her to Swedish Medical Center, which was not distant, and I followed in my car. The doctor in the emergency room checked her vital signs and said he could find nothing unusual. He asked about a history of epilepsy. Machiko said no one in her family had ever had an attack.

Finally the doctor said I could take Machiko home but advised that we should go to our regular family doctor for a thorough checkup. Then, almost as an afterthought, he said, "Oh, one more thing: I recommend she get an MRI—you know, a magnetic resonance imaging that will give the doctor a look at her brain."

By coincidence we had an appointment for a checkup scheduled two days later with our family doctor. By then Machiko seemed to be quite normal. The doctor found nothing unusual but sent us to see a neurologist. "Just in case," he said. Some extensive tests were taken. Again, negative.

All went normally until about a month later. While Machiko and I were working in the garden, I heard her cry out, "It's coming."

I rushed to her side and helped her to lie down on the grass. "It's like the last time," she said, "like an electric shock."

"I'll call 911 and get you to the hospital," I said.

"No," Machiko said. "I'll be all right. Let me rest a moment and then help me into the house."

The next day, our doctor sent us to another doctor, who specialized in problems with facial nerves. He found nothing unusual.

Machiko put on a brave front but was unusually quiet and her appetite dropped. So far our doctors had been unable to help her. Even though she felt well, she understandably was in fear of another mysterious attack.

One day early in March, Machiko awoke early and went into her office to work while I caught a few more winks. Presently she came back into the bedroom. "I can't work the word processor," she said, anguish in her face. "My left hand keeps hitting the same keys." The next day she lost control of her left hand and leg.

Once more we went to the neurologist, and this time he ordered an MRI. The same day, we took the results to a brain surgeon.

His face was grave as he spoke to us: "Normally, in case of serious surgery, I recommend a second opinion. But I'm afraid you don't have the time to get one. There is a cancer growing in your brain. Your life is in danger and we must operate without delay."

Two days later Machiko underwent brain surgery. The date was March 18, 1998. A large malignant tumor was removed, but the surgeon could give me no assurance that he had been able to take out all of it.

Machiko came through the operation remarkably well. She was in good spirits and talked about returning to work and meeting the next deadline for *Understanding Japan*. But the radiation and chemotherapy that lay ahead were to subject her to the most excruciating period of her life.

The chemotherapy involved commuting to the hospital for intravenous injections of powerful drugs for eight hours a day. After three days she was exhausted. The doctors gave her a twenty-four-day break before giving her four more days of chemotherapy. After the fourth treatment, she was so exhausted that she had to be hospitalized for a time. Nearly a month later she was started on a third chemotherapy series, remaining in the hospital this time because it was too hard on her to travel to and from home. When she had recovered somewhat from the chemotherapy treatments, Machiko started radiation therapy, which lasted thirty-three days. Throughout the ordeal she was a good soldier. Her will to recover amazed even the caregivers.

Miraculously, Machiko began to feel better. She said she was anxious to resume working on *Understanding Japan*, but by then I had decided we had to discontinue publication. Yet we could not simply drop the project. Our subscribers had paid in advance and were entitled to refunds. Letters were sent to all of them—with Machiko helping to stuff the envelopes—explaining our problems and offering to send them checks for the unexpired portion. It was gratifying that many subscribers wrote back to refuse a refund, express their sympathy, and urge us to resume publication when we could.

In June, three months after her surgery, Machiko had a welcome visit from two of her sisters, Reiko Matsuta and Teruko Okada, both educators. She was strong enough to take them out in the back yard to display her flowers, and enjoyed being pampered when she was resting. After the sisters left in early July, Machiko told me she was growing weaker. Soon nausea started and she was unable to keep down the pills that had been prescribed. Another MRI showed the cancer was coming back. She had her second surgery on July 17.

This time something new was tried: her brain was treated with a light-sensitive dye and a laser beam was used to attack malignant cells that could not be reached by conventional surgery. Exposed to ordinary light, the dye would become toxic. I had to take Machiko home after dark, where all the lightbulbs had been replaced by fluorescent lights. By the time the dye lost its toxicity, Machiko was well enough to go for short strolls.

One day she told me she would like very much to visit Japan and felt she had the strength to make the trip. Her doctor told me to go while she was stable because, he warned, she will grow worse. We flew out of Denver International Airport on a bright September morning with return reservations in three weeks. The flight was easy and pleasant. Machiko enjoyed the meals and slept when she was tired. Airline attendants with wheelchairs helped us at the terminals. Relatives who met us at Narita Airport expressed surprise at how well she looked, and I don't think they were just being nice.

For ten days Machiko enjoyed herself immensely, demonstrating a remarkably good appetite for favorite foods she had missed and visiting with relatives and old friends who came to visit her at the hotel.

On our tenth night in Japan the nausea started. I gave Machiko pills that stopped the nausea, but I knew I must lose no time in getting her to a doctor.

And by great good fortune I knew exactly whom to call.

CHAPTER 18

"Never Give Up"

NOT LONG AFTER MACHIKO'S FIRST OPERATION I had received a telephone call from a friend, Randy Dybing. He had worked for a period in Japan as a representative of an American firm, but was now living temporarily in Golden, near Denver. Dybing said he had happened to visit the JETRO Denver office and had heard about me and Machiko's illness.

Dybing went on to say he had fallen ill in Tokyo and had been referred to Dr. Kiyoshi Sato at Juntendo Hospital. There his problem had been diagnosed as brain cancer. He had undergone five operations at Juntendo, Dybing said, and now he was feeling perfectly fine.

"I owe my life to Dr. Sato," Dybing said. "If you are ever in Japan, I urge you to take your wife to see him. And tell her, never give up. Never. There always is hope."

I thanked Dybing and jotted down Dr. Sato's name, just in case.

Now, I thumbed through my memo book, found Dr. Sato's telephone number at the hospital, and called him.

A woman who identified herself as Dr. Sato's secretary said he was in Australia and asked how she could help me. I told her who I was, that I had been told about Dr. Sato by an American named Dybing, and briefly explained Machiko's problem.

"Oh," she said, "Dr. Sato is the director of Juntendo. He is scheduled to return tomorrow. And even though it's Saturday, I know he will come to the office. I will ask him to call you."

Dr. Sato's telephone call came Saturday afternoon. I thanked him profusely and explained the circumstances.

After he heard my report he said: "It would be very helpful if I knew more about her medical history. Could we get the records from her doctor in America?"

"Dr. Sato," I replied quickly, "I have copies of all the documents here with me."

"Fax them to me right away," he said.

Several hours later he telephoned again. "Bring your wife to the hospital at 9 o'clock Monday morning." That would be September 21.

Most hospitals in Japan are relatively small and owned and operated by a physician or group of physicians. Juntendo is famous for its ophthalmologic department as well as for surgery.

Dr. Sato turned out to be a slightly built man in his middle years. He had a gentle, friendly manner and a twinkle in his eye. I felt a confidence in him. There must have been a mountain of work awaiting Dr. Sato after his trip but he spent the morning with Machiko. She was admitted to the hospital that very afternoon.

Dr. Sato explained that Dr. Osamu Okuda and his team of five physicians would be placed in charge of Machiko's case. Dr. Okuda, he told me, had studied several years in a Chicago hospital. He also told me something I had known but dreaded hearing: medical science knew no way of killing the cancer. "All that we can hope to do is to keep her as comfortable as possible," he said. "I am very sorry, but she will grow progressively weaker and there is nothing that anyone can do about it."

Inside, I wept.

About two weeks after entering the hospital, Machiko underwent a third operation. Dr. Okuda explained that the main purpose was to create space for the tumor, which was continuing to grow rapidly. The operation would not cure her, but would make her as comfortable as possible.

I asked a question that had been bothering me for a long time. When Machiko suffered her first attack, the emergency room doctor had suggested that an MRI be performed. But that wasn't done for some weeks, not until after she had suffered a second attack. Would an MRI immediately after the first symptoms have revealed the cancer in time to effect a cure?

Dr. Okuda shook his head sadly. "No," he said. "Even then it would have been too late, and because of the nature of the tumor and its location, I do not know that a surgeon's knife could have reached it in any event."

The nurses and other attendants at Juntendo were amazingly kind, gentle, thoughtful, and cheerful. Machiko loved their attention and because she was so appreciative they gave her even more affection. Dr. Sato and a retinue of doctors and nurses would make the rounds every Monday and Friday afternoon. Machiko looked forward to their arrival because they were so pleasant. Sometimes I would help her into a wheelchair and take her outside for some fresh air. And when she felt well enough, she would interpret for American patients.

"I want to go home," she told me one day. "There is so much I want to do." She wanted to resume *Understanding Japan*. She wanted to take on more book projects and looked forward to working with schoolchildren.

But that was not to be. She grew progressively weaker and eventually I took over the responsibility of spoon-feeding her.

During her last several weeks she was in a coma. She died on June 28, 1999, nine months after entering Juntendo. There was cremation and in a quiet ceremony her ashes were placed in the Sogo family tomb in Tokyo.

Several weeks later I returned to the empty house in Denver. Our friend Kathy Ajisaka had been looking after it. The lawn was trimmed and the place looked much the way it had when we left nearly a year earlier. But of course everything was different. It would never be the same, even though, when I set out the seed and table scraps again, Machiko's beloved birds, squirrels and foxes returned.

On July 21, 1999, some of our friends gathered for a memorial service at the Denver Buddhist Temple to bid Machiko farewell.

Postscript

AS ITS TITLE INDICATES, THIS BOOK IS THE STORY of my efforts as a public relations specialist working for better understanding between the United States and Japan. I could not tell the story without saying much about JETRO, the Japan External Trade Organization, which was the vehicle through which I worked for thirty-three years. It was not easy to relate my story without appearing to be a spokesperson, or an apologist if you will, for JETRO, which sometimes has been condemned as an official agency trying to justify Japan's allegedly closed markets. That was far from my objective.

However, I have no hesitation in endorsing what JETRO has accomplished, which is promoting international trade.

In a sense JETRO logically may be considered a form of international philanthropy in the same way that many private companies and corporations donate time, money, and expertise to improve their communities.

With Japanese taxpayer funds, JETRO at first promoted exports that helped lift the national economy from the disaster of war. These exports met some of the needs and improved the living standards of many nations at a time when the world was hungry for quality goods at reasonable prices. But when Japan's export industry became able to stand on its own, JETRO changed its focus to seeking a more equitable trade balance by promoting imports to Japan. Much of my story has to do with my efforts in this direction.

International trade has contributed vastly to raising living standards around the world. There can be no more worthy endeavor. Inexpert and bumbling as my contributions were at the start, I am proud I, and Renko and Machiko, were part of that effort.

Appendix

Japan's Trade Balance						
	With the World			With the U.S.		
Year	Exports	Imports	Balances	Exports	Imports	Balances
1945	0.9	2.2	▲1.3	—	—	—
1950	8.2	9.7	▲1.5	1.8	4.2	▲2.4
1955	20.1	24.7	▲4.6	4.5	7.7	▲3.2
1960	40.6	44.9	▲4.4	11.0	15.5	▲4.5
1965	84.5	81.7	2.8	24.8	23.7	1.1
1970	193.2	188.8	4.4	59.4	55.6	3.8
1975	557.5	578.6	▲21.1	111.5	116.1	▲4.6
1980	1298.1	1405.3	▲107.2	313.7	244.1	69.6
1985	1756.4	1295.4	461.0	652.8	257.9	394.9
1990	2869.5	2348.0	521.5	903.2	523.7	379.5
1995	4429.4	3361.0	1068.4	1208.6	754.1	454.5
2000	4792.8	3797.2	995.6	1424.7	721.7	703.0

(unit = $100 million) ▲ = negative balance

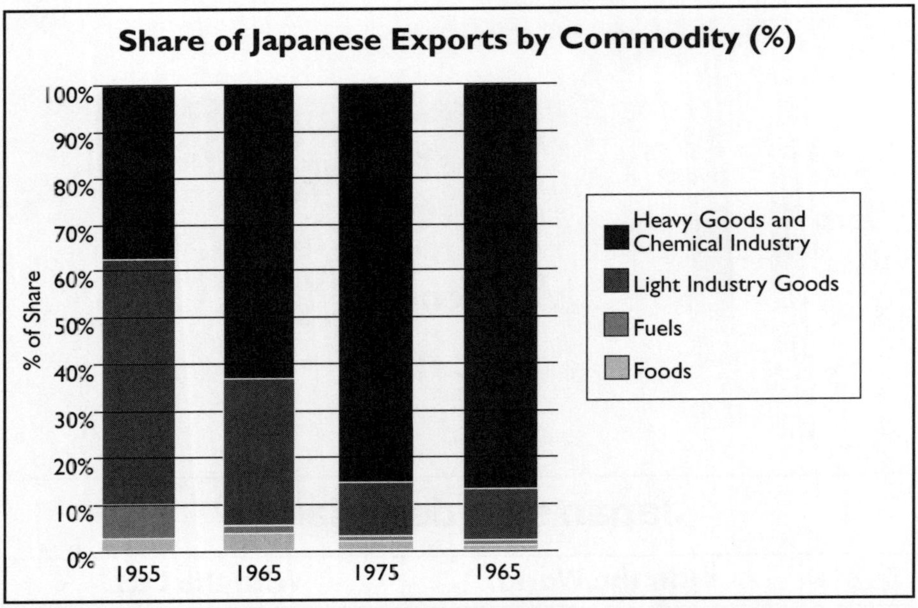

Source: Ministry of International Trade and Industry (MITI) White Paper

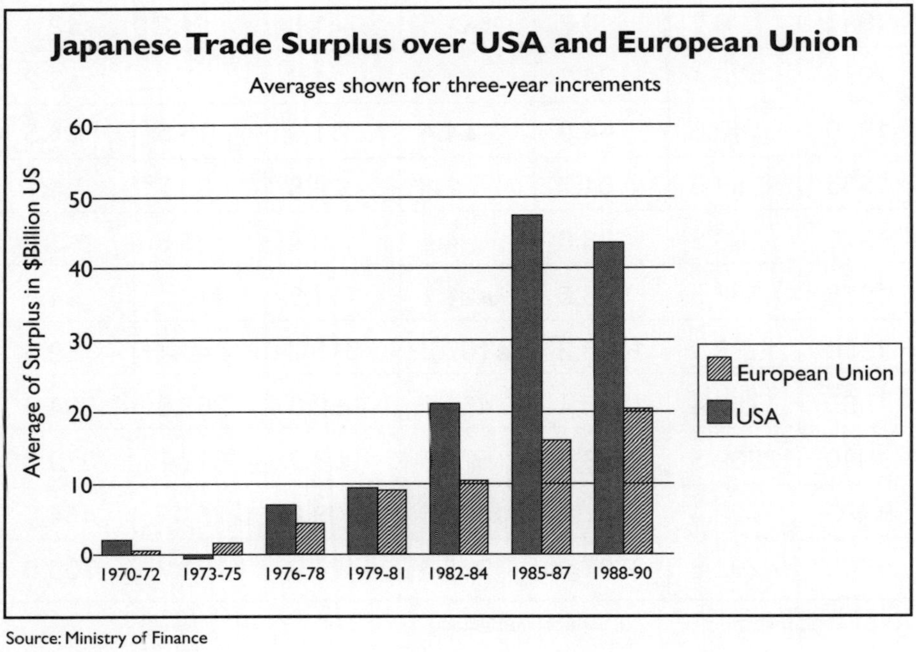

Source: Ministry of Finance

Transition of Japanese Imports by Industry

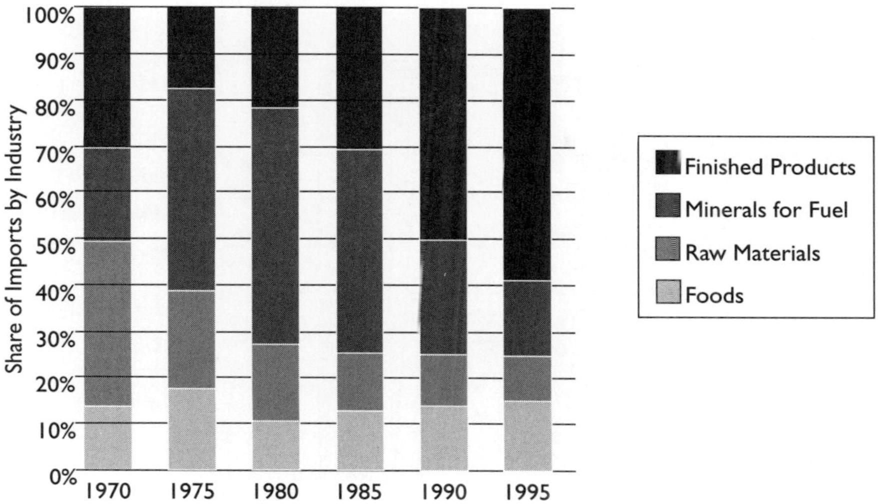

Breakdown of Finished Products (from above)

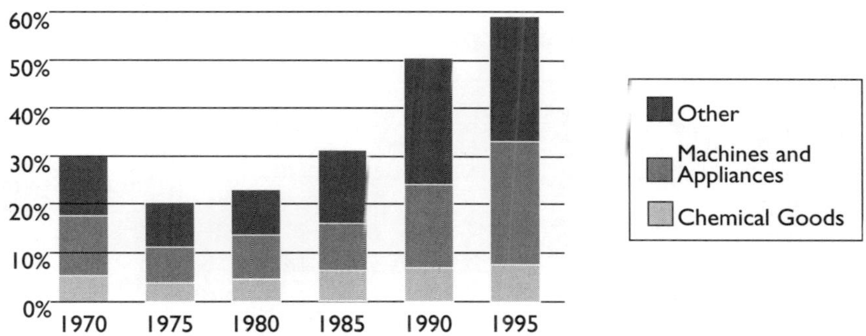

Source: 1995 and 1996 JETRO White Paper, International Trade Section

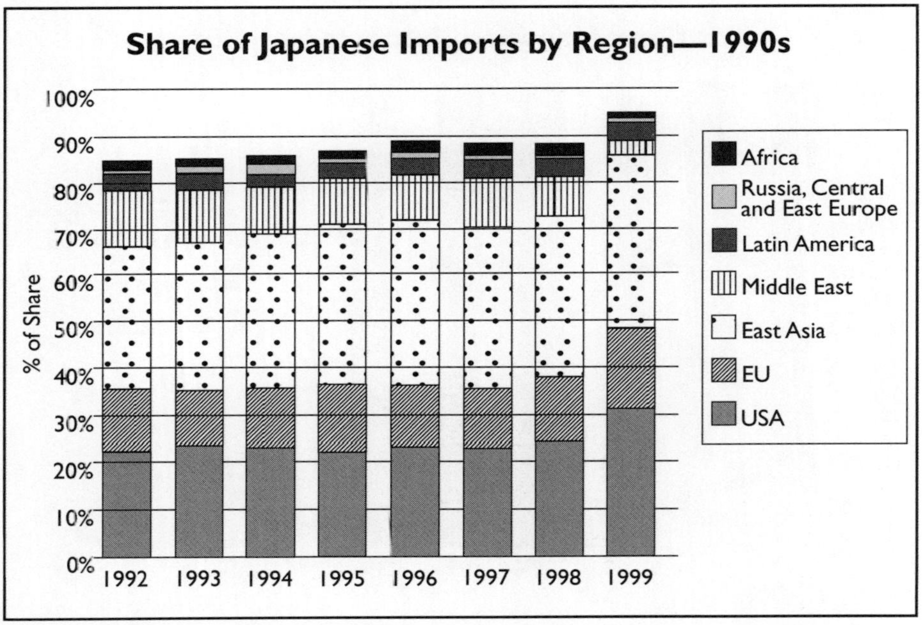

Source: JETRO White Paper on International Trade

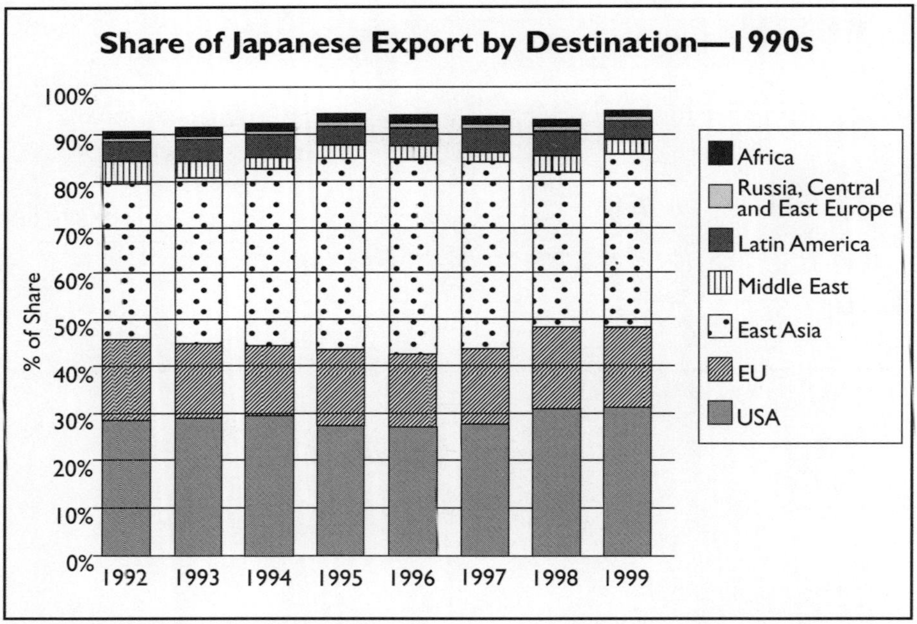

Source: JETRO White Paper on International Trade